JERSEY: NOT QUITE BRITISH

D1642536

'Bertha and piglets' – see Introduction

JERSEY:
Not quite
British

*The Rural History of
a Singular People*

David Le Feuvre

Illustrations by Pat Miller

SEAFLOWER BOOKS

First published in 1993
Reprinted in 1994 by
SEAFLOWER BOOKS
16½ New St. John's Road
St. Helier
Jersey

Seaflower Books is an imprint of Ex Libris Press,
to whom all enquiries and correspondence
should be addressed:

EX LIBRIS PRESS
1 The Shambles
Bradford on Avon
Wiltshire
BA15 1JS

Typeset in 10 point Century Schoolbook

Design and typesetting by Ex Libris Press
Cover printed by Shires Press, Trowbridge, Wiltshire
Printed and bound in Britain by
Cromwell Press Ltd., Broughton Gifford, Wiltshire

ISBN 0 948578 57 2

CONTENTS

Introduction

FOR A WHILE it seemed a good idea to set down my own memories as a smallholder farmer in Jersey, and of a system of agriculture which had existed in the Island for centuries. It was not that my experiences were at all remarkable but rather, so it seemed at the time, that unless somebody provided it before an ageing generation had finally passed away there never would be a permanent record of a kind of farming and of an agrarian culture that were in many ways unique to the Island and which finally all but disappeared during Jersey's unrecorded postwar agricultural revolution. There was plenty to write about.

There were Solonaise and poor, arthritic Rush's Rosebay, the first cows we bought. They were housed for a while in a stone-floored shed near the kitchen door while we rebuilt the stable which, in the years that followed, was home for many others. There was, for example, Chloe, in every respect bar her crumpled horn the best cow we ever had and whom I found one morning dead in the field with her prematurely-born heifer calf dead alongside her. And there was Belinda, a relative of Chloe and an animal of equally elegant breeding who finally went to live in the United States.

There was Bertha the sow. She was called Bertha because in the early hours of a night of snow and bitter winds she gave birth in the farrowing pen to a litter of eleven young. In those postwar years when meat was still scarce one of the litter was fattened and finally slaughtered amid screams that sounded to humans like infectious, sickening fear. The corpse was cut up and parts were salted in the stone trough in the bakehouse. Once matured, the joints were wrapped in cheesecloth and hung in the coach house, where despite the craving for meat they swung for months in passing breezes and grew a blue mould because we recalled the death and could not bring ourselves to eat the hams and sides of bacon Bertha's child had provided.

There was Bob the horse, alone in his dark, cobble-floored, sweet-smelling stable. Imported, probably from France, during the war, he seemed to understand English well enough; but although amenable he was lazy. On the days when he did not feel like work he would put his head up tight against the whitewashed rafters of the low stable so that to slip the collar over him became a battle of wills and strength. On several occasions when harnessed to the ancient cart, only brutality would have made him pull it after a half-hearted lurch on the tug chains made him decide that it was too heavily loaded, so that the manure or mangolds had to be tipped in a heap Bob could see and then some part of it loaded again.

There were, of course, the Breton workers, upon whom at that time Island farmers depended almost entirely for their labour. Little, serious André, for example, who while working in the fields tried to teach me Breton while I taught him English. He said one day that he understood all the BBC weather forecasts on the wireless bar the bit which spoke about 'Margaret zu gut c'est la bella day'. It seemed an attractively polyglot remark. I went with him to listen. "It says 'moderate to good visibility', " I told him afterwards. From then on we lost interest in each other's native tongue and spoke French instead.

There was the gang of four, three men and an old, black-garbed lady, who came as seasonal workers for the potato season one year. At first the men drew enough cider from the barrel in the cider room to leave them constantly fuddled. For a week the digging went at a snail's pace. But each lunchtime the old lady secretly poured jugs of water into the barrel. As the cider grew steadily more diluted, so did the rate of harvesting increase. By a rare stroke of good fortune, that year the price of early potatoes rose on the English markets instead of falling. Thanks to the cider we had the most profitable season I can remember.

There were Joseph and Marie, whose conjunction of biblical names I recall because they seemed so inappropriate. They behaved like insatiable honeymooners to the point at which, a doctor being called, it was suggested that for her own good Marie should return to France while Joseph remained with us and physically distant from her. I often wonder what happened to them, as I

8

wonder what became of Joachim and Rosalie, two of the nicest people one is likely to meet. I hope they finally did build the house whose design they had even put on paper and which they showed me with such determined pride.

As I recall her, Rosalie was not so much pretty as downright beautiful. One summer's day, pregnantly heavy with the threat of thunder, Joe was carting the bundled hay while Rosalie and I were working in a loft redolent with the heady perfume of a crop as soft and enfolding as a mattress and where, suddenly, I was taken with a lust for her: Even now I sometimes wonder whether, by that mysterious chemistry of thought, she felt as I did, for the longing could do no other but remain in my mind.

Of such things are memories made. Of sowing oats by hand, striding with a strange feeling of exhilaration over land Bob and I had harrowed; and of seeing, a few weeks later, the miracle of a million tiny spears of shoots turning the soil from brown to a green that became more evident every day. Of sitting unprotected on a tractor, ploughing, while snow turned my greatcoat white and white seagulls wheeled and cried; and of rows of freshly-harvested potatoes as richly gold as anything that could be dug from King Solomon's mines, and richer by far than worthless gold itself. Of milking in a warm stable on a cold day with my head resting against a soft flank while the milk hissed and bubbled into the traditional spherical Jersey pail.

*   *   *

As I wrote, the memories came tumbling out unbidden, as they do now. But in the end I gave up. I could not make the story work. There were several reasons, but chiefly it was that what was appearing on the page seemed more and more to be nothing but a disagreeable exercise in nostalgia and self-indulgence. It might have become a marketable product but it lacked the truth I wanted to tell.

Farming is not, and can never be – as some authors try to portray it – a matter of romantic emotion. It was certainly not in that light that their daily lives were viewed by those like myself who were working the land; nor was it as I viewed it at the time.

Romance, always a product of the past, can never tell the truth. There is winter rain and bitter wind from the east, there are ruined or failed crops and market gluts, droughts, animal diseases, employment problems, quarrels and disputes, times of great despair.

Above all, so far as the kind of smallholder farming about which I was trying to write was concerned, there was at that time too often the unremitting physical work which on occasions could leave the mind numb and the body exhausted and from which neither a diminishing pool of labour nor the kind of machinery then available, nor even sufficient capital, could ease the burden or provide a means of escape.

*   *   *

That attempt proved to be a dead end. But it had a value. It encouraged me to look beyond the narrow horizons of personal experience, and back into history itself for a broader view of things. It slowly became more clear to me than it had before that I had been an active witness during its last years of a system of smallholder farming that was in many ways unique and among people whose culture, equally unique, stretched back through the centuries. There grew the urge to provide a record of an imprecisely documented past.

I discovered that for much of its history as a part of what finally became the British Isles the people of Jersey had lived lives remote from the rest of Britain. It was not until the early 1800s that the English began to arrive, first as wealthy immigrants and then as tourists. Up to that point the Island's population – its rural inhabitants together with their transient seafaring relatives and those who were in trade – had formed a distinct and unassimilated people. They spoke their own language, they governed themselves, they had their own social orders, their own traditions and history, their own laws, their own particular characteristics. They were as close to being a separate nation as any small community might expect to get. They were certainly not English, nor French or even Norman, nor yet entirely like the natives of the neighbouring Bailiwick of Guernsey. They were truly a singular people.

For those who opted to stay on the land rather than taking

to the sea, theirs was a way of life which had evolved in its own fashion over the centuries that followed the Norman Conquest, although with surprisingly few sudden changes. It is that slow evolution, together with the ability of the people to adapt to changing circumstances and to seize opportunities when they present themselves, which shines through Jersey's rural history, as it does of the Island community in general, just as much in the past as in more recent times.

A knitting industry which grew to astonishing proportions and which thrived for over two hundred and fifty years took the Jersey smallholder from mere subsistence farming into the profitable world of commerce. The export of woollen goods, particularly stockings, was followed by a cider industry so great that Jersey was described on one occasion as being 'a sea of liquor'. Then, in the early 1800s, there came that great era which made the Island breed of cow internationally famous. Cattle and the Jersey Royal early potato, first exported in the late 1800s, formed a marvellous partnership and brought considerable wealth to many an Island farmer – as did, for a while, the outdoor tomato.

Slowly, too – for it takes time for the mind to assimilate such things – I came to realise that the Jersey countrymen I knew who still spoke the Island's ancient language, and were in thought and deed so often unlike those other members of a rapidly increasing Island population, were in fact the remnants of a particular kind of people whose fate was to be absorbed into a new order.

It was a fate sealed by Jersey's agricultural revolution which came silently but inexorably in the decades after the Second World War. Changing circumstances both within the Island and far beyond made the revolution inevitable. Locally, the boom in tourism which came with peace, and the explosion of the finance business in the 1960s, toppled agriculture and its allied industries from the prime positions they had so long held. In the broader sense, changing economics meant that there was no longer a place for the smallholder with his few vergées of land devoted to a system of mixed farming.

In the postwar years Jersey, increasingly anglicised and urban, has continued for better or worse to prove its vigorous sense of commerce and desire for profit and to demonstrate its ability

11

both to adopt and adapt. But at the same time it has witnessed the decline, and perhaps even the actual loss, of a particular form of agriculture, of a particular culture based on rural values, and above all of the distinctive presence of a breed of native Jersey- man, born free, independent and without the benefit of States help or the brake of States control, whose life was centred upon his land and what his land produced.

*   *   *

As I read and researched, it became clear that those who had written about Jersey in more recent times had never set out intentionally to explore what seemed to me to be the most fun- damental of all the subjects – the character of the native people and the industries which brought great prosperity to what had essentially been a rural Island; and if they had, it was too often in a negative, dismissive way. So it is such people and the products of their labour which form the basis of this book.

The first part offers a general, perhaps simple and certainly incomplete view of the historical events which played a part in creating the nature and temperament of the native Jerseyman.

The second part deals briefly with that most important of all Jersey's natural resources – the land – and the way in which it was at one time cared for and cosseted to the point where it became so fertile that it could produce crops abundant enough to keep even small farms viable.

The third section explores the growth and decline of those industries whose exportable products – knitted goods, cider, cattle, potatoes and tomatoes – brought prosperity to the Island for many generations and enabled smallholder farming to flourish long after it had been swept away in most other parts of the British Isles.

The meticulous may take the critical view that in places opinion replaces fact. If that is so, I make no apologies. On occasions I have had to go down new paths without the benefit of guidance from others who had gone before, and on occasions I have had to rely on supposition and deduction. In doing so, I have laid myself open to disagreement and perhaps error. Besides, even the most precise historical record involving human affairs must necessarily be influenced to an extent by the judgments of its author. And, I suppose, a book composed solely of facts is no more appetising than potatoes without salt.

Nor do I apologise for the fact that the hugely important subject of Jersey's mercantile commerce and those who owned and sailed in Jersey ships, as did many of my ancestors, is virtually ignored. True, they form one half of the Island's history. But to have tried to encompass both the sea and the land in one volume would almost certainly have resulted in the kind of academic tome more useful to the serious historian and researcher than attractive to the ordinary reader whose interest I have set out to engage.

Those who wish to know more about the Island in a general sense could do no better than acquire Balleine's *History of Jersey* revised and enlarged by the late Marguerite Syvret and Joan Stevens. Without frequent references to it, and to other publications of a lesser stature, this book could not have been written. Nor could it possibly have reached this stage without the help and steady encouragement of Jurat Max Lucas, whose knowledge of the Island, its agriculture and its country folk deserves recognition. He has written the last chapter of this book, which provides a brief comment on Jèrriais, the ancient language once used by all the Island's inhabitants.

I doubt, too, whether I could have found the courage to persist had not a supportive family left me alone to get on with it.

But if there is to be a dedication, it must be to those who once were a truly singular people, les vrais Jèrriais.

They deserve a memorial
Not lest they be forgotten
But because they
Have never been known

PART ONE

*The Character
of the People*

1.
Members of a British family somewhat apart

THE REV PETER HEYLIN visited Jersey in the early 1600s. Afterwards he reported that 'the peasants were inclined to a kind of melancholic surliness, living in poverty and marrying within themselves like conies in a burrow'.

Those were the days when there were no doubts in the minds of reverend men of God and those of high estate. The Almighty had ordained that there should be differences and distinctions between them and those of the lower orders such as the peasants. The two, while all of the human race, were separate. The one was superior, the other inferior, as it had always been and would be. And although it was the clear duty of their betters to make the inferior classes happy and contented with their lot, it was by no means the wish of the Almighty that they should strive to regard the peasant as being their equal. The attitude deserves momentary emphasis since it has coloured the reactions of so many writers, all necessarily educated men, to the less educated countryman of old. It is a view that has softened over the centuries. Now it is not as it was in Heylin's day. But it still remains, a mere grain which nevertheless casts a vast shadow over our perception of the country dweller in days gone by.

The shadow is clearly evident in R.C.F. Maugham's *The Island of Jersey Today*. Published in 1939 and revised as late as 1950, there is nothing in it to suggest a sympathetic understanding of the rural population in the place where he chose to live. Maugham, pictured on the frontispiece in uniform with cocked hat, sword and much gold braid, came to the Island in the 1930s as what is now called a wealthy immigrant. While he loved Jersey

16

and approved of the 'official, professional and commercial classes', and no doubt of the golfing, bridge and cocktail party society he mixed with, he had not one kind word to say about the native farming stock. 'With regard to physiognomy the expression on the countryman's face is rather stolid and his manners not very ingratiating,' he reported. The women 'though occasionally comely, are not, as a rule conspicuously well favoured...nor are they outstandingly endowed with natural grace and movement.' They also tended, like the men, towards 'steatopygy', which is to say big behinds.

Concerning their character, said Maugham, 'the lower classes cannot be described as temperate,' while 'as in country districts on the Mainland morality is a virtue not very highly regarded. Illegitimacy I understand to be common.' Basing his views on sketchy details of ancient migration patterns, he argued with the contempt accorded to the Jews at the time when he wrote that the inhabitants must have been of Semitic origin. 'If any additional reason for such a supposition be needed,' he remarked, 'it would be found in the Jerseyman's deep-seated attachment to money-making.'

Maugham reserves some of his most scathing criticisms for the difficulty he obviously had of finding reliable domestic servants 'of Jersey birth'. No problem, of course, for those who could bring staff with them when they moved to the Island or among those for whom 'the sordid details of household management are confidently left to the housekeeper'. For others less fortunate 'it is possible, however rarely, to obtain the services of more or less uncouth country damsels; but the continuity of their engagement is always rendered uncertain, not to say improbable, on the approach of the potato and tomato seasons.' Then, or if a better offer arrived than the £2.10s a week they might get as domestic servants, 'they often absent themselves without even the almost empty formality of the usual week's notice, leaving their overwrought employers stranded and helpless.'

He was obviously upset also by their lack of deference to their employers, likened by another author writing some time before Maugham to the take-it-or-leave-it attitude to be found among the employed in the United States.

17

Maugham was a product of his background and the climactic era of a dominant and absolute British Empire. He was one of many who, on retirement after serving overseas, decided to settle in Jersey. Although it was a part of the British Isles, despite the lack of servility among the natives it still provided the satisfying feel of the distant dominions this ruling class had grown used to.

*   *   *

Right from the period in the 1800s when steamships, unlike sail, began to provide reliable links with the United Kingdom, the Island's differences, its beautiful coastline, its rurality and its cheapness made it an increasingly attractive holiday resort for a growing middle class with money and time to spare.

Add to its other attractions a lack of oppressive laws on taxation and inheritance and the absence of the kind of worrisome social and political problems to be found in the rest of Britain, and it becomes clear why many also saw Jersey, as Maugham did, as an ideal place to live permanently in retirement. Not surprisingly, the numbers grew and developed into the kind of enclosed colonial coterie of English men and women one might have found in some far-flung British dependency. Indeed, for a time the Island was noted for its impressive corps of retired Navy and Army officers as well as former officials who had served in distant places.

It is estimated that as early as 1840 there were five thousand English residents. They lived apart, refusing even to speak French, still the language commonly used by many of the more educated of native Islanders. As one guidebook writer of the mid-1800s put it: 'The English society is quite different from the native society. I do not say they never mingle, but the intercourse is limited and infrequent.' Maugham himself sums up in awful detail the daily lives of these wealthy, ageing immigrants – one might almost say refugees – as it was in his own day. 'A visit to St Helier in the mornings to lay in cigarettes or fill up the petrol tank, followed by a call at the club; a cinema, bridge or a round of golf in the afternoon as the prelude to a cocktail party, and finally, dinner, more bridge, and so to bed.' It was the kind of exclusive group the better class of inhabitants might be invited to enter but only a favoured few became a part of; the lower classes not at all.

Maugham's views deserve attention, for they indicate the attitudes of some retired people who came to live in Jersey. Many – although by no means all – of these English immigrants brought with them a sense of superiority, rather as victors will who settle in a conquered land. And while each may well have done much that was good in his individual life, it has to be said that, as with the Army officers of the English garrisons once stationed in Jersey, they altered Island society and tended to divide it. Although many welcomed their presence, they also left behind a legacy of unexpressed resentment that was particularly evident among the ignored country people. It is a view which lingers on.

That attitude may have been misguided but it was – and maybe still is – understandable. For while such people might have been totally absorbed easily enough into a community in some rural part of their homeland, Jersey was too different for that to be possible. They remained, as it were, foreigners on home soil; as some still do.

Perhaps unwittingly, Maugham himself provides the reason. Although loyal to the Crown 'the people of Jersey,' he said, 'have never regarded themselves as anything but Jerseymen, almost to the exclusion of all else, and to this distinction they have, of course, every right to cling. But however curious it may appear, it may be said that even today it does not seem that most of them look upon themselves as, in every sense of the term, members of the British family, or, if they do, it is as members of a branch of that family somewhat apart.'

*   *   *

Another Englishman, who came to Jersey over a century and a quarter before Maugham, formed a quite different opinion of the rural population. John Stead paid a short visit in 1809 and later wrote of his impressions in *A Picture of Jersey*. Stead had the arrogance, temper and snobbishness of a true Georgian; yet in his writing he anticipated the cloying romanticism of the Victorian era whose writers, painters and poets so often saw in the countryside and its inhabitants an idyll, an Arcadia, which of course

19

had never existed. In that sense he was like his contemporary, the great William Cobbett. And like Cobbett he seems to have been an endearing, peppery, observant sort of man.

His voyage from Weymouth in the *Rover* packet took place sixteen years into yet another intermittent war between Britain and France which was to end in Napoleon's defeat at Waterloo in 1815. Not surprisingly, therefore, he noted with obvious satisfaction that the vessel 'carried several carriage guns besides small arms so that neither Row Boats nor Privateers had any chance of capturing it.'

Much of Stead's *A Picture of Jersey* is just that. It includes descriptions of his various tours, of the homes of the more illustrious residents he passed and of an Island remote in almost every way from anything we can now imagine. Uncritical, he seems to have liked all he saw. He was particularly attracted on his tours of the countryside by the 'innumerable Cottages built in that firm style which convinces the observer the Erector built not only for himself but for his Posterity'.

At the time of his visit to Jersey the cattle trade was in its infancy and the great era of knitting was beginning to die, brought to an end by the Industrial Revolution and changes in fashion. But woollen goods, together with great quantities of cider, were still the Island's main exports. Stead reported admiringly: 'Knitting is the chief employment of the Women. The Dexterity and Expedition with which they dispatch a pair of stockings are almost incredible. To them Light and Darkness are indifferent. A Woman seen walking without a Stocking in her hand is stigmatized with Idleness'.

Ever ready to detect symptoms of rural bliss, even of bucolic jollity, he noted: 'In Summer (the women) assemble in large Numbers, and sit in a ring under the Trees which make of all the roads a continuous Avenue; and the avocation must be urgent that can call them from the social Party.' Come the winter, groups of knitters gathered at neighbours' houses where 'seated on soft Rushes carefully picked and dried for that Purpose.... from the close of Day to Midnight an universal Activity prevails. Nor let it be imagined that these hours are dull and tedious. They indulge their native Mirth in innocent Recreation and the song of Festivity forbids the intrusion of Melancholy.'

It is easy enough even now to picture these social evenings, *veilles* as they were called in Jersey Norman-French, then the natural language of the Island and of the rural people in particular. At these gatherings knitters would sit together on the great *liets de fouaille* – large couches covered in straw or bracken – which were then a feature of many of those homes which had damp earthen floors or floors of cold Swanage stone. They were held in the dim light of a tallow candle or two, or maybe from cressets whose wicks, floating perhaps in the oil from the livers of locally-caught fish, provided an uncertain – and certainly smelly – atmosphere. It is no wonder that country folk in Jersey, as in so many parts of the world, believed implicitly in the kind of tales of the supernatural and of witchcraft that must have been told, over and over again, amid the dancing shadows at social gatherings like these.

They had one particular benefit, these homely working evenings. According to Stead: 'The young Men, returning from their more hardy Occupations of the Day, repair to these cheerful meetings. There, seated in the Middle of the Ring, they pay their Offerings at the Shrine of Beauty and yield their Souls to the Impulse of Love which is here attended with an Innocence and Simplicity unknown in larger Countries.'

Stead writes of the rural inhabitants of Jersey with a sympathy that was quite unusual for his time, although with that cloying sentimentality that outdoes truth itself. 'Amongst the native Inhabitants,' he noted, 'conjugal and domestic Blissfulness exists in all its primeval excellence. Unions are founded on Affection and cemented by an unceasing Earnestness to promote the Interest and Enjoyment of each other. The Welfare of the Family is the predominant study of the Parents...and...the Children love each other from the Example of their revered Relatives.'

*   *   *

Stead's book has been described as the first tourist guide to the Island. As Jersey became more accessible, other books followed. Some, like Henry Inglis's *The Channel Islands*, published in 1835, are investigative, factual and interesting. Others, like Maugham's, were handbooks written almost exclusively by English people for the benefit of English people thinking of visiting on holiday or settling in Jersey. While it is true that there exist many documents written by Islanders which help to provide a picture of ordinary life in former days, it is only in recent times that some have appeared in published form. Moreover, they were the product of those who had the benefit of enough education to read and write, and the time and inclination to do so. So far as the many very ordinary Jerseymen who made up the bulk of the population of an essentially rural Island in former days were concerned, that was rarely the case.

So it might seem that if there was at one time what interested readers could regard as a reliable and consistent source from which to learn a little about the country people as they were in the 1800s and even before, and the kind of lives they lived, it should surely be from books such as these. After all, one might suppose that the authors could not avoid making some friendly contacts with the inhabitants on their travels. But clearly, like Maugham, they did not. If one had to pass judgment now merely on what most of them had to say, the country folk enjoyed few redeeming features. Yet it was the attitudes of these authors which formed the basis of a general view of the local population. As history knows, rightly or wrongly once formed these opinions tend to become permanent fixtures.

To quote some impressions of the country people gleaned from the books by English authors writing in the 1800s. They were generally 'unprepossessing in their physical appearance'. They were short, even squat. The women 'by reason of continual toil from the cradle lacked the elegance consonant with their sex'. As for the men, they had the gait of ploughmen, ungainly manners and the 'coarse features so frequently found among those who work the soil'. They were dressed without thought for style. 'Somehow or other – it is difficult to say why – their clothes generally look as if they were cut out with a pick-axe and put on with a pitch-fork.'

Much of their clothing was fashioned at home, the country tailors being, not as elsewhere, men but women who worked for

5d a day. The tailor was not always called upon, of course. 'The dress of men and women is of worsted which has been subjected to the knitting needle...not only stockings and shawls but petticoats and even small clothes.' The women's apparel was usually sombre. 'Through inter-marriage a great proportion of the population is constantly in mourning, many of the females in the country always wearing black bonnets to be ready to meet the oft-recurring season of wearing black.'

They worked unendingly. Several reports make this dedication seem not so much a virtue as a deadening fault. While in England men were still abed, complained one writer, in Jersey lights could be seen early every day in the houses throughout the countryside. Not only were they industrious. Even worse, their industry was said to be accompanied by a lack of merriment and jollity. The only exceptions, it would seem, were at the appointed seasons of *vraic* (seaweed) gathering when numerous groups, often using small boats, set out to harvest the weed attached to inshore rocks. Then something approaching a picnic atmosphere prevailed, as it did at the corn harvest when, it was said, the harvesters sang *les chansons de moisson* which were described as 'repetitive and inappropriate' songs.

They were mean; not so much careful as plain miserly. 'A Jerseyman will do anything but put his hand in his pocket,' protested one writer. Another remarked: 'I have heard it said that a sick man would rather remain ill than enjoy a broth made from one of his best chickens which he might sell in the market for 1s. 6d.' A third wrote pointedly: 'Where there is independence of character and action there may be found avarice and parsimony.'

Judging from reports, their food was simple in the extreme, easily prepared, unendingly the same at every meal and entirely home grown. It consisted – or so it was claimed – of bread usually baked every fortnight and *soupe à la choux* or *soupe à la graisse*. The ingredients of the former were cabbage, parsnips, turnips or potatoes, the latter also containing fat pork, all boiled in a cauldron suspended over a fire, often of dried vraic, smouldering in the kitchen's open fireplace. Maybe now and again there would be a little fresh or salted pork or perhaps conger eel soup.

While they were honest – about the only good trait generally

'Their food was simple.'

remarked upon by writers – by implication they were surly, inhospitable and uncivil to strangers.

None of the authors of these old books, not one of whom appears to have been born in the Island, seems to have understood Jersey Norman-French, still the universal language of the countryside, or wished to. It was described either as 'that terrible jargon' or a 'barbarous dialect of French'. Nor did many of Jersey's townsfolk speak the ancient language of the Island. By the time these books were written most spoke English or French rather than the language of their forebears which provided a living link with a past that stretched back to the time of William the Conqueror and probably before.

There are two reasons why remarks of this kind deserve to be used as an introduction to any inquiry into the character of the Jersey people. The first is that they tend to reflect the attitudes of the authors and the times when the Island and what would have been called its 'peasant stock' were first written about in a serious way. The second is that what can now be thought of as judgments biased by those attitudes inevitably played a large part in forming opinion among a wide sector of the British and Jersey public.

Obviously Jersey's farming folk had as many faults in former times as any other. But the mind recoils at the picture which emerges as one reads these books of a community composed of such unremittingly awful, not to say stolid, taciturn, ungracious and unappealing people whose sole claim to approval was honesty. True, they were industrious. If not an inbred characteristic, it was certainly one upon which their prosperity depended. They were careful with their money, perhaps to the point of being miserly. It is a trait still attributed by some to the Jersey people. What caused the critics to regard penny-counting as a shortcoming rather than a trait deserving praise is difficult to say. Certainly it was a quality which must have enabled some of the writers to find the funds and the freedom to visit the Island. On the other hand, a dedication to high fashion was not one of their interests. Working people did not – do not – usually worry too much about demonstrating their social standing by means of sartorial elegance, or about the niceties of cuisine.

It may be that they were not much given to frivolity, at least not in front of strangers. The Jerseyman has always borne more of the dour temperament of the Nordic and Teutonic people than the feyness of the Breton Celt or the vivacity of the Latin. Besides, those who know Jersey Norman-French, 'that terrible jargon', will be aware that it is a language well suited to the kind of robust humour usually restricted to intimate gatherings and so not generally recognised by outsiders.

More inclined to the dumpy than the slender, it is very probable that the Islanders' bodies reflected the times when medicine was basic and uncertain, and existence depended on hard physical toil. Even today the life expectancy among people in the poorest countries is still little more than forty-five. No doubt in past times that was how it was in Jersey, as it was elsewhere.

Beyond doubt they were unresponsive when approached by strangers who seem to have treated them as they would subject members of a lower order who could not, would not, speak their language – and who may blame them?

So, with the benefit of hindsight and that more sympathetic attitude they so obviously lacked, it becomes evident that the authors of many of these books had little understanding of Jersey's farming stock when they expressed such harsh disapproval. All too often they observed them through the eyes of the English town dweller and by the urban standards by which they lived at a time in history when England's rural Hodges and Jorrockses, like the urban labouring class, had become set in the mind of an expanding educated middle class as artless figures of fun ripe for disapproval and mockery.

All wrote with unfailing delight about the Island itself. It was entirely consistent with the period in which they lived that they should then go on to dismiss the less educated men, women and children they saw in it as country bumpkins and no more than disagreeable accessories to romantic rural scenes.

As a later chapter will explain, social and economic upheavals in the late 1700s onwards had tended to turn a whole class of English countrymen who had once been cottagers enjoying a degree of freedom into mere labourers. They poured on to an overcrowded labour market. It was not surprising that such people quickly learnt that survival depended on subservience to their betters; and more to the point, that their betters could come to require their servility.

In fairness, therefore, it might be said that it was impossible for the kind of people who were in a position to visit the Island in former times to accept that in Jersey many of those they saw as scruffy, vulgar individuals were not in the least servile – in fact, quite the opposite judging from what was written about them. Had they made further inquiries they would have learnt that despite their appearance many were landed proprietors and freemen on however small a scale. Theirs was a society based to a great extent on self-employed men and women among whom submissiveness to a master had never been any part of life's experience.

One writer had the insight to remark: 'It must always happen that where men cultivate their own land and labour for their own profit, a certain independence of character will be engendered.' Thus those who came to Jersey and later wrote about it for the benefit of their own class arrived in the Island cocooned in the false belief that the local community, and in particular the country dwellers – who during the era in which they wrote prob-ably still formed the greater part of the native population – could be expected to be a mirror image of what was to be found elsewhere in the British Isles.

Of course nothing could have been further from the truth. In a sense Jersey was, and conceivably still is, 'an island entire of itself'. Between them, geography, history and history's natural bedfellow, chance, combined to create a population which, though minute, once had characteristics and a manner of living unlike any other; rather as secluded families left to their own devices will tread their own paths and create their own tiny traditions and attitudes that are different from those of their neighbours.

Reading these books, one is left with the amusing but not quite ludicrous image of intrepid Victorian travellers coming in a great forest upon some previously undiscovered tribe of ancient lineage. They stand – men, women and children – in a circle, their arms linked and each facing inward towards the others, entirely self-contained in every respect, in their language, their traditions, their nature; content with what they know and what they are, and quite heedless of those who peer inquisitively and without the competence to understand from outside the circle which they can never enter. As an analogy, that is ominously exact. For in the end, as history knows, it is always the tribe, not its discoverer, that is finally vanquished.

And so it happened in Jersey.

2.
King John puts the overlords in a fix

JERSEY'S HISTORY comes in small pieces rather like an interlocking jigsaw puzzle. Alone, each seems to have little relation to all the others. Put together, they make a picture that is unique. Each piece has played some part in creating the character of the Island's natives both as individuals and as a community whose roots reach back through the centuries. But it is a jigsaw puzzle which seems to work in reverse; to recognise the appearance of the completed picture one has first to understand at least some of the bits from which it is made.

* * *

In the long ages before travel became easy and communications rapid, the inhabitants of small island communities usually enjoyed a particular and peculiar sort of advantage. They were remote from the centres of oppressive authority, and central governments tended to leave them alone to run their own affairs. That kind of freedom was reinforced in Jersey's case by the first of many fortunate chances.

It came in 1066 when the Island, as part of the Duchy of Normandy, found itself on the winning side. In due course the victor at Hastings, Duke William, died; and in the years that followed his heirs, while retaining control over their ducal lands, made what was to become England their permanent home. Things went well until King John took to the throne. By 1204, in one way and another, he had lost pretty well all the overseas territories, including that part of the Duchy of Normandy which lay on the Continent.

This posed serious problems for those barons who held land in the Channel Islands. Up to that point they had continued to pay homage to the man they knew as the Duke of Normandy. But by this time the Duke had become the King of a new country called England, from which an equally new country, France, had quite suddenly become separated as a result of John's losses to Philip II. So now the barons had to decide; should they side with Philip and France (and so retain what other territories they held on the Continent) or risk all and remain loyal to John and England – and in doing so, hold on to what they held in the islands?

For obscure reasons, although no doubt with their thoughts fixed firmly on their own likely advantage, the more powerful overlords of the Channel Islands, now situated within sight of a potentially hostile Normandy, decided to stick with the English Crown, distant though it was. It was a decision which enabled King John, through the allegiance they offered, to confiscate those other areas of land in the Channel Islands held by other and less powerful men still resident in Normandy who had decided to join the opposite side. Not surprisingly, he awarded them to his supporters. In that way, of course, he rewarded those who had remained loyal while at the same time guaranteeing the undivided fidelity of the people of this distant part of his kingdom.

The decision of the overlords to side with King John represents the first of many examples of the good fortune from which Jersey has benefited over the centuries. For had the decision gone the other way, the people of Jersey would almost certainly now be French and inhabitants of an island of little significance tied to the rule of the French government.

While it does historical accuracy no great credit, the foregoing is at least a simple outline of the facts. But then matters become a little less clear. What seems obvious is that King John, either on his own account or through his officials, had little choice but to repay the loyalty the Channel Islands had shown in some practical way. He did so (tradition says, although some historians disagree) by granting them a specific constitution which gave them certain privileges and rights, including that of governing their own internal affairs and of trading with England without having to pay English duties. It was a wise move. The one gave them a welcome degree of freedom, while the other provided a vital bond between these distant islands and the British mainland.

If there ever actually was a Channel Islands Magna Carta, it disappeared long ago. Quite likely there was something written on parchment, for in 1248, thirty-one years after King John's death, a Royal Commission was appointed to inquire into the islands' constitution and legal system. In point of fact these may have existed long before King John's time – even before the Normans invaded England – through slow development rather than through any decisive act by him. However it was, the commission decided – or reaffirmed the decision – that the islands should be free from all English military service, taxes and imposts and confirmed the constitution as it existed in the time of King John, which presumably included that of managing their own internal affairs.

*　　*　　*

Since then, of course, things have changed. The centre of power has moved from the Crown (the monarch, however, remaining titular head of state) to the Houses of Parliament. Paradoxically, while the islands remain dependencies of the Crown, it is not the Crown but Parliament – where the Channel Islands have no elected representatives – which now has the ultimate authority to act on their behalf in matters relating to the British Isles as a whole, or to interfere unilaterally and directly in local affairs should that be thought necessary.

The most recent judgment on that always contentious issue was made following a Commission of Inquiry into the Constitution of Jersey in the 1970s. The Commission concluded that 'so long as the United Kingdom Government remains responsible for the internal relations of the islands and for their good government, it must have powers in the last resort to intervene in any island matter in the exercise of those responsibilities'. So far, although pressures may have been brought to bear from time to time, that has never happened.

The fact is that the islands' relationships with the United Kingdom government are convoluted and defy any logical and simple explanation. As they currently exist, they could no more be incorporated into a written constitution than could a long-standing gentleman's agreement. They are based on an understanding of history, a mutual respect and a continuing, although now largely academic, allegiance to the Crown.

What emerges is that throughout the course of the past seven hundred years and more the constitution granted (or confirmed) in King John's time has remained unaltered. Within the limits of common sense (which is perhaps the essence of the thing) the islands retain their ancient right to trade with the rest of Britain without payment of duties, to the right to govern their internal affairs, to raise taxes and to pass their own laws (but always with the prior consent of the sovereign given during formal meetings with his – or her – Privy Councillors).

Whether the Channel Islands will be able to maintain unchanged that unique freedom in face of those judgments by the European Court of Human Rights which are all-embracing, and of the decisions of the European Community which are extended to the islands, is another matter. Be that as it may, the point is that there is nothing like belonging to a small, sea-girt community which has enjoyed such a high degree of immunity from outside control for so long a time to ensure an inborn sense of pride in that belonging, and a personal desire for independence from others. If that is true of the people as a whole, it must surely tend to be just as true of the individuals in it.

*   *   *

The point has already been made that in former times the people of most distant communities were more or less left to themselves. But so far as the Channel Islands were concerned that was not entirely the case. Since they lived in vital southern outpost fortresses facing France, Britain's almost continual enemy, not only did the inhabitants need to be kept loyal by giving them special privileges, but the islands themselves, together with their excellent harbour facilities, also had to be defended. Even today the British authorities retain the responsibility for matters relating to the defence of the islands. Indeed, until quite recently they were heavily guarded at all times by garrisons of British troops and local defensive forces – citizens' militias – in both the Jersey and Guernsey Bailiwicks that had been in existence even before the Norman Conquest. However, apart from its strategic position and its invaluable attachment to the Crown, Jersey was for centuries not a place of any particular significance in civil terms. The native, left to administer his own affairs, was allowed to plod on is way without too much direct interference so long as he did not cause trouble. There was certainly no reason why anybody, apart from the local population, should choose to live in the Island. The British troops, for example, did so only because they had to.

What need was there among those powerful Englishmen involved in the affairs of state, but above all with their own advancement, to consider a few thousand ignorant peasants who spoke some unintelligible lingo and who lived days and an uncomfortable sea journey away from the core of government, a proximity to the decision makers and the givers of favours? Typically, many of those appointed Governor chose not to reside in Jersey. Having received the honour – at some cost in return for this favour – together with the income that went with it, they then went on to engage some lesser person to take their place as Lieutenant-Governor to be resident in the Island, paying them a proportion of what they themselves received from the British government.

Sir Walter Raleigh was a case in point. As one of Jersey's Governors (these days the most famous but by no means the best) he spent only two months in the Island during his three years in office; an appointment terminated abruptly when he was arrested in England, confined in the Tower of London and finally executed. Possibly the permanent loss of his head in 1603 was a fate he might have avoided had he remained contentedly in office in Jersey instead of swashbuckling about in the Americas.

Apart from a Governor, or his appointee, and the senior officers of the British garrisons stationed in the Island, there was no special advantage for anybody hopeful of advancement in taking up anything but temporary residence in Jersey. Nor, of course, for those concerned with trade. There was little enough of that and certainly not more than could be handled by local men of commerce noted for their business acumen. Jersey was regarded as some-thing of a dead end.

*   *   *

There were exceptions to this general lack of immigration. Among those who arrived and settled were the Protestant refugees, the Huguenots. Many fled from the oppressions of a Roman Catholic France both in the 1570s and the 1680s to a nearby haven where French was spoken and which had been greatly influenced by the kind of French Calvinistic Protestantism whose beliefs were the cause of the Huguenots' persecution. It was, moreover, an uncompromising, unadorned kind of religion that seemed to suit the character of the Island people and which undoubtedly played a part in their enthusiastic adoption later of Methodism and perhaps even in making the Jerseyman the kind of person he came to be.

Indeed, one wonders for a moment whether, given all the facts and allowed a vote, the ordinary people of Jersey really would have agreed to play host to that rich, distinguished and flamboyant royal refugee, Charles II, and his wealthy entourage, favouring instead the sober simplicity of the Royalists' enemies, the Parliamentarian Roundheads.

Many of the Huguenots settled in Jersey permanently. Most were men and women of severe conscience and considerable intelligence. They brought with them money, a degree of education and, as often as not, valuable craftsmen's skills. Jersey profited from their presence just as much as did the Huguenots from the protection it provided.

Generally speaking, though, right through the Middle Ages and into Tudor times – and perhaps well beyond – the sea, the language, the way of life and the fact that apart from its maritime trade Jersey was a place which had not much to offer but subsistence farming, all tended to be barriers to immigration. There was little cause for English people to move to the Island and every reason why the neighbouring French should not. There must have been exceptions. But in the main – and despite the Island's international trade – its rural inhabitants remained remote from intrusions of any kind.

If there was a reluctance among the English to move to this distant and uncoveted part of the British Isles, there must also

34

have been just as much of a desire among some of the more alert, spirited and intelligent natives to get away. Very probably a proportion of the brighter young men left the land to go to sea or to seek their fortunes in distant places. Others, expecting only a minor inheritance from the family smallholding, also decided to emigrate. After all, until quite recently in Island history there were no fortunes to be made from the land, no chance of adventure or excitement. Instead – as many of those who had little hope of benefiting from a parent's wealth may well have thought – there was the kind of pettiness and malicious gossip endemic in all enclosed communities, a lifetime composed of a dull, repetitive round and the suffocating restraints that come with living close to families and relatives.

In the absence of sharp historical or statistical fact it has to be a matter of opinion what effects the general absence of non-native blood, the slow haemorrhage from the Island of some of the more enterprising, self-reliant natives, and inter-marriage among Island families, had between them on the inherited qualities of such an enclosed community and on Island society in general in the centuries before the influx of English residents and the arrival of the tourist trade.

There are those who will argue forcefully, and with good reason, that it had none. As proof they will point (as examples) to the continuing vitality of the Jerseyman through the ages, his ability to adapt easily to change and to profit from it, and to the many Island-born men and women who became famous, or wealthy, or both. Degeneration, they will say, is not necessarily a consequence of isolation. On the other hand there are those who will argue with equal vigour, and on the basis of modern genetics, that the result of close breeding between families, human or otherwise, will usually lead to the fixing of certain attributes – some of which may be valuable while others, although not harmful in themselves, may not always be beneficial.

So complex and controversial a subject is one best left to the expert to investigate; but not one to be ignored here entirely for that reason. For if the people of the Island – that is, those with Island-bred forebears – have certain jointly-shared characteristics, some part of them must surely be due to inheritance. And

35

if the effects of character and temperament are pervasive enough throughout a community, it must surely be reasonable to suppose that they tend to influence the kind of place Jersey is even now, and the atmosphere it has.

*   *   *

Trying to give an impression of affairs from late medieval times to the present day, even in a sketchy and imprecise way, is difficult enough; and not more so than attempting a brief but vital outline of the Island people's relations with mainland France.

At the time of the Norman Conquest and for a very long while afterwards they could hardly have bothered about the fine points of nationality since it was a concept that barely existed. So far as the Jersey peasant was concerned he knew exactly where he stood. He spoke the language of his kin, the neighbouring Normans. He had ancient family and trade links with Normandy.

The newly-conquered island to the north – once the land of the Anglo-Saxons, a quite different race of people – was a distant, foreign place. It lay somewhere over the horizon and just on the edge of understanding. It played no part at all in his life. If he owed allegiance to some person outside the sphere of his existence it was to the successors of Duke William of Normandy, no matter where they happened to live. By slow degrees, of course, that had to change. Jersey stopped being a part of the disintegrated Norman empire and became instead a possession of an English Crown often at war with what was turning into a fairly unified France.

Perhaps what made the people of Jersey most clearly aware of the fact that they were now detached from the nearby Continent came at those times when Frenchmen invaded the Island. After all, by definition he who invades becomes an enemy. Among those who did so with more or less success were Bertrand du Guesclin in 1373 and de Maulevrier in 1461. The latter succeeded in taking Mont Orgueil, the one real bastion of local defence, announced that he was Lord of the Channel Islands and held some, or maybe all, of the Island for the next seven years. There was probably not much fighting and few deaths among the population. But by their action such men and their ragged armies became recognised as opponents to be hated and feared rather than as brethren.

However, these dramas, important though they were in their times, could have had little direct effect on the lives of the peasants. The average man and woman went on having a difficult enough task getting born, living for a while, procreating and dying without bothering too much about which side they were supposed to be on.

*　　*　　*

Well into the 1700s and certainly later, proclaimed enemy or not, it was with nearby Normandy that many of the Island's population continued to maintain the closest links. For a long time England remained a kind of *terra incognita* about which they knew little and cared less and never dreamed of visiting. It was Normandy, with its fairs and markets and its known language, that was the attraction. There one could buy and sell, meet friends or often distant relatives, enjoy oneself and quite probably get very merry in the liberal atmosphere of such events.

For obvious reasons, then, little of whatever character and attitudes the English nation may have been developing through the Dark Ages and onwards rubbed off on Jersey's country people, even if they did on the seafarers and the better educated. They remained more French than English in their thoughts and their way of life. Maritime commerce and conflicts apart, France, through Normandy and a common tongue, continued to be the individual country dweller's chief link with the outside world. But of course matters could not rest there. By slow turns the whole of the Island's population and not just a section of it began to assimilate certain British ideas and start to recognise its Britishness as something permanent and complete. Maulevrier's invasion over, wars and dissensions on a larger European scale continued to encourage the slow growth of loyalty to Britain. The French, always at the doorstep and often threatening once again to land on Island soil, came – like the British nation of which they had grown to be a part – to be seen as a distinct and separate people.

It was a strange period in Jersey's history. On the one hand France was a foe. On the other, relations with Normandy, although

37

not France itself, remained on a friendly footing. The people went on speaking a kind of French similar to that of the neighbouring enemy while English, the national language, continued to be barely understood. The attractions of old friendships and profitable business with nearby Norman ports and towns were set against the opposite forces of enmity and fear. Privateers made some part of their living by capturing enemy vessels, smugglers by means of friendly contacts. Both operated in the same stretch of water. Finally, of course, the slow accumulation of differences and a strengthening attachment to what was seen at last as the 'mother country' made it inevitable that even the most untutored and ignorant among the Island's population should lose whatever sense of dual nationality they may once have had.

*   *   *

By the start of the nineteenth century the Jerseyman was no longer Norman and certainly not French. He was British and either accepted the fact or was proud of it. Contacts with France and its people became looser and at a less personal level until the time came in the late 1800s when peasants from Brittany, then a poverty-stricken region largely ignored by the French authorities, began to arrive in increasing numbers. They became essential cogs in the Island's hugely prosperous and labour-intensive agricultural industry. For their part, they were only too pleased to earn money by helping with the potato, hay and corn harvests or as permanent farm workers. But they were regarded with a certain disdain, and not just because of their ragged appearance and clumsy manners. By this time the French were well and truly foreigners. To say that a man was French was frequently not a neutral statement of fact but rather a means of showing a reluctance to welcome him into local society. Even in recent times to marry a Frenchman was as much a disgrace in certain quarters as a Protestant marrying a Roman Catholic.

This apartness was reinforced during the 1800s by the increasing numbers of English immigrants and tourists. While Jersey-Norman French remained the language of the countryside, French itself was coming to be spoken less and less by a diminishing number of people in everyday life, and then it was usually for commercial reasons. Although many in the town were bi-lingual, there was neither much need for French nor any great desire to speak the language of a people who lived within sight of the Island but who had to be treated with caution.

*　　*　　*

Like those developments in the nineteenth century which did so much to forge even closer links with Britain, the introduction into Jersey in 1912 of compulsory education brought many benefits, especially for the children of some parents who could not afford to pay for private schooling and the offspring of others who continued to hold strong views on encouraging too much brain and not enough brawn.

At the same time it played a part, for good or bad, in breaking down a remarkable internal language barrier which had grown up as the result of the slow anglicisation of Jersey. There came to be two quite separate groups. On the one side there were those, mostly in the urban areas, who spoke English as their natural tongue. On the other there were those, mainly in the countryside, who were brought up from infancy to speak in Jersey Norman-French and knew little if any English. It is not stretching the point too far to suggest that the latter tended to be the true Island stock whose attitudes and temperament were those of their forefathers.

Despite that, for perhaps the next forty years many hundreds, and most probably thousands, of these country-bred youngsters started their education at parish schools where, at the outset, they were quite unable to understand the language used to teach them. They became, in effect, tiny confused foreigners in their own land. What in some respects was even worse was the fact that the country child who left school at fourteen often did so with only a limited vocabulary and accents which frequently led – as they still do – to taunts that they were by nature stupid and of a lower social standing.

Speaking Jersey Norman-French was forbidden both in the classroom and the playground. No formal attempt was made to teach those young pupils English and they were obliged to acquire

Trinity School, early 1900s

it as best they could. They learnt history as seen through the eyes of the English and absorbed English traditions and culture; but none of Jersey's. From one point of view, although it was brutal, abrupt and insensitive in a way that would now be thought intolerable, judging by the needs and the less sophisticated standards of the day it could be said that there was no other choice. Although French remained the traditional language of the States and the Royal Court, English and Latin had for centuries been the languages of education in Jersey.

Reflecting the attitudes of the times, the Education Committee of its day could not have thought Jersey Norman-French to be other than the valueless, archaic tongue of peasants who needed to be dragged into the modern world. Anyway, there were not enough qualified teachers who were able to understand, never mind speak, the natural language of many of their pupils. From another point of view it was a shameful period in the Island's history. Wrong though such a claim must surely be, it was almost as though a considered attempt was being made by incomers to impose their language, their standards and their urban ways on the ignorant *originaires*.

Thus much of an ancient way of life was done away with by the simple expedients of ignoring the glue of language and of educating children in a way which took no account of their ancestors' past.

* * *

It has been said that the 'invasion' of the English, personified in particular by those who wrote so scornfully of the country dweller, did more harm to Jersey than did the Germans during the years of the Occupation. It is an absurd suggestion. But from one perspective not entirely so. The advent of English immigrants and English tourists and men of business among so isolated a community had a profound effect on the fabric of Island society. As with the Indians of the Americas, for example, or the Maoris of New Zealand, or the aborigines of Australia, a fragile social and cultural balance was upset. Lacking experience of resistance, the Jersey country man and woman slowly came to believe themselves

41

to be inferior; were vanquished, subjugated and finally absorbed into a new order of things imposed by others.

It is no wonder that there were so few complaints over the imposition of the English language on those natives who could not speak it. Protesters would at best have been ignored, at worst accused of obstructing their children's education. Besides, while vanquished people will complain among themselves, they seem by nature to be unable to contemplate actual mutiny. No doubt the anglicisation of Jersey has been unavoidable. One cannot proudly proclaim that one is British and enjoy the benefits of being so yet not accept the facts and consequences of Britishness.

So – barring commercial activity – what had once seemed the Island's indissoluble links with France had been all but severed by the time compulsory education arrived in Jersey; to be restored to an extent, and in a quite different form, in more recent times by tourism, tolerance, personal friendships and a new sense of internationalism.

3.
All I know is
I had a cow

AN ANCIENT ATTACHMENT to Normandy was one reason why the character, temperament and attitudes of Jersey's rural population failed for so long to match those of similar kinds of people in most other areas of the British Isles. The Island's remoteness and insignificance were others, its history of independence a fourth. But the biggest gulf appeared during what has come to be called the Industrial Revolution. It was an era which probably saw the greatest ferment of social change in the shortest possible time in the whole of British history. It was not principally about the machines of which technically-minded writers make so much. It was about people.

This bloodless social revolution spread with furious energy outward into the rural areas as surely as it did into the expanding urban centres; and in doing so demolished a rural way of life and altered English agriculture for ever. The connection between these events and the character of the Jersey people demands a brief explanation.

Until this time a proportion of England's countryside had been held as huge estates by men of long-standing wealth and power, the successors of the feudal barons. A part was cultivated by yeomen farmers, once the knights of olden times. Most of the remainder of the land was in the hands of freemen who lived interdependently as smallholders in village groups. At the outset of the revolution the pattern of these cottagers' lives and the kind of agriculture they practised remained as they had done since before medieval times; and, indeed, as they had done in Jersey until the introduction of a cash economy based on knitting. Each owned a few acres of land as separate strips in several huge, unenclosed fields that were cultivated communally. Corn – usually wheat, barley or rye – and beans were the only crops grown in these open fields. It was on the corn harvests that the cottager depended for the greater part of his food and to pay, in kind, his dues and tithes to church and lord. In addition, he held joint rights to the surrounding common land – rough, uncultivated areas where pigs, geese and cattle could be grazed and wood gathered for fuel.

So it was the English cottagers who constituted the greater part of the rural population in a rural kingdom where at that time the kind of sprawling cities we know today just did not exist. They enjoyed what might now be called a steady-state economy that was self-supporting and self-perpetuating in almost every sense and was totally dependent on the land. There was little call for money – for the itinerant tinker, maybe, or the travelling seller of cloth and trinkets. But the tiny amounts of cash which came from selling at the nearest market what few items were produced in excess of a family's needs played only a small part in their lives.

All, or nearly all, of this settled way of life was swept away within the space of a few generations by the onslaught of the Industrial Revolution. A freedom that was based on land ownership, a subsistence economy and sometimes the existence of small cottage industries was lost to the demands of a cash economy based on centralised industries. As part of this upheaval there came a concept previously unknown to most country dwellers – that of a permanent employer and his attendant, and dependent, paid employee.

It is said that between 1750 and 1810 some four thousand Acts of Enclosure were passed, and probably the same number of enclosures came about by private agreement. Some two to three million villagers are thought in one report to have been involved and up to twenty per cent of agricultural land in England and Wales. Another puts the figure at some three million acres of farmland – one hundred times the area of Jersey. Yet another suggests that the figure was as much as seven million acres. Whatever the true amount, the greater part of this enclosed land was lost to the peasant smallholder and passed into the hands of a new breed, the large commercial farmer bent upon improvement and profit.

44

In human terms the upheavals in agriculture characterised by the Enclosures, and the rapid urbanisation of many areas in the United Kingdom, spelt misery and degradation for what had formerly been rural families who, previously, had led simple but sufficient lives in the countryside as cottagers confident that food they had grown, basic though it might have been, could always be found for the table.

Their situation was summed up by the Rector of Cookham in Berkshire. David Davies wrote: 'For dubious economic benefit an amazing number of people have been reduced from a comfortable state of partial independence to the precarious condition of mere hirelings.'

*   *   *

No doubt this era of rural change was as necessary as it was predestined by the flow of British history. It had many supporters, among them Arthur Young. Yet he was able to write with evident regret that thousands of Englishmen could say: 'All I know is, I had a cow, and an Act of Parliament has taken it from me.'

That was not a lament that would have been heard in Jersey. The revolution which was taking place on the distant mainland did not, could not, export itself there. For one thing there were no mineral resources to exploit, no cheap source of power nor a pool of cheap labour. For another, for over a hundred and fifty years before the start of the Industrial Revolution the Island's rural population had been involved with its own quite profitable export businesses. While the trade in knitted goods and cider making will feature more fully in later chapters, it might be said here that they truly were cottage industries ideally suited to Jersey and its own different way of life.

By their natures – and perhaps by the independent nature of the people themselves – they could not be transformed and gathered into centralised factories using permanent paid labour. Nor did they encourage urbanisation. Indeed, both depended for their success on the existence of family units and the kind of smallholder farming that, as in England, had survived for centuries and was to continue to do so in Jersey for another hundred and fifty years despite the upheavals that had occurred in the United Kingdom. Thus while the Industrial Revolution proceeded with such devastating effect in distant England, the pattern of life in Jersey remained unchanged simply because there were no external forces to make it do otherwise.

As to any kind of rationalisation of land ownership, there was neither need for that nor any possibility. Jersey had begun to move away from the medieval practice of strip-farming open fields on a communal basis several centuries before the start of the Industrial Revolution. And although there were still large areas of jointly owned and uncultivated commons, they were slowly being eaten into as more was taken over by individuals for planting profitable cider apple trees and for arable farming.

Well before the 1700s almost all of the cultivated land in Jersey had become separately owned, enclosed and quite intensively worked as fields reached by many twisting tracks which evolved into unpaved lanes and finally the narrow roads which are still so much a feature of the Island's countryside. By the English standards of the times these fields were ridiculously small. One reason for that was the Island's inheritance laws, whose effect was a tendency to carve up already tiny estates into yet smaller parcels. In theory at least, the consequences of death could have divided and divided them yet again into patches too minute to be workable. But common sense intervened and a kind of stability was reached that prevented patches being turned into mere plots.

So, long before the great revolutionary changes which occurred in England, Jersey farming had settled into a comfortable, and seemingly unchangeable, pattern based on the existence of a surprising number of individual and quite separate smallholder units. They were owned and worked by the Island's equivalent of the English cottager in the sense that families were usually able to remain independent and to support themselves from what they grew or the livestock they raised.

But there were differences. For example, as far back as the 1500s Jersey's smallholders, unlike their English counterparts, had begun to move from mere self-sufficiency to a cash economy based on the production for export of knitted goods. Later, cider and then cattle sales provided them with an increasingly substan-

'Fields reached by many twisting tracks.'

tial cash income. Besides, landowners were rarely tempted by changing circumstances to part with even a fraction of their precious soil.

There were no villages such as one might have expected to find in England, no clusters of houses, no sense of huddled togetherness. It is surely a mark of the Jersey character that the many properties dotted around the countryside stood isolated among their own fields, each one an entity in its own right. There was, of course, a sense of communality. Almost without exception these many small, distinct and separate holdings were run by families, but they could always depend on relatives or neighbours when extra help was needed. As late as 1858 one writer, Edward Gastineau, reported: 'Jersey agricultural labour is not generally to be hired for there is a kind of give-and-take system among the natives by which they assist one another when aid is required.'

Thus at the start of the Industrial Revolution, Jersey's internal economy – such as it was – provided very few opportunities for employment and none for the expansion of industry as the word came to be known in England.

* * *

Estimates of the Island's population in the days before censuses come from various sources. It was put at being in the region of 12,000 in 1331. In 1634 it was thought to be 25,000 but in 1646 it was believed to be over 35,000; thirty-nine years later it was claimed by one writer to be not more than 20,000 and by another 15,000. Whatever the true figure may have been at any one time – and certain authorities put the figure for most of the 1600s and 1700s at about 20,000 – nearly all those who were not involved in maritime affairs were connected with the land and had some land of their own.

Writing in 1835, Henry Inglis referred to '...that largest class of the natives who are at once proprietors, occupiers and labourers of the soil. This is, with few exceptions, the condition of all the country people. Their possessions are from two to three vergées up to 20 or 30 vergées.' (A vergée is the Jersey land measure. An acre contains 2½ vergées. The area of a small football pitch measuring one hundred yards by sixty yards would be 1.2 acres, or 2.7 vergées)

To those whose knowledge of agriculture is limited to farming in England in the present day, it must seem astonishing that a family could exist, never mind gain a living, from such minute areas of productive soil. But like the English smallholdings which had been lost in the flood of change in the late 1700s and early 1800s, they were pretty much self-contained units. The family provided the labour and grew its own food on land it owned. Diligent and careful by nature, the people had few wants which exchange, work for others or the sale of the goods they produced could not satisfy.

Moreover, unlike most of their English counterparts they were able to enjoy the harvests of the sea in the days when the inshore waters abounded with fish and shellfish in a way they no longer do. Many families even had their own small craft. For the Jerseyman there was no division between the land and the sea. In fact so far as the Island's smallholders were concerned theirs was such a successful way of living – and profitable thanks to hard work, kindly soil, the crops and livestock it supported, the waters around the shore (and good fortune) – that it persisted with little change until the Island's agricultural industry underwent its own revolution in the early 1960s.

A reliable picture of Jersey farming does not appear until 1930 with the publication by the Department of Agriculture of the first of a subsequently annual set of statistics. Despite the move to larger holdings in most other areas of the British Isles, they show how little had changed in the size (and therefore number) of smallholdings since the time of Inglis a century before and almost certainly for generations before that.

There were (in round figures) 1,800 farms in Jersey, the area of land cultivated being something over 46,000 vergées – or an average size of holding of only twenty-five vergées. In fact, of the 1,800 farm units, nearly a third were of between one and ten vergées, while only 199 were of fifty vergées or more. Few English families could hope, or anyway enjoy the opportunity, to support themselves on such tiny parcels of land. But then, even in so recent a past as the 1930s, conditions in the United Kingdom, where agriculture was far more extensive and depended less on human muscle, were quite different from those in Jersey, where intensive cultivation had for so long been the basis of the agricultural industry.

Statistics are dry, boring things. However, one can at least use them to capture an idea of the level of physical labour involved on these small Jersey farms where every square yard of the land was valuable. Even as late as the third decade of the twentieth century there were 1,600 horses but only seventy tractors on the 1,800 smallholdings; and while there were nearly 12,000 head of cattle the use of milking machines was not thought worth mentioning until 1952.

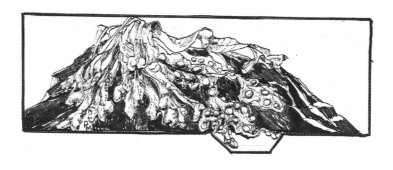

4.
The cream of society and the hungry poor

THE ISLAND'S SOCIAL structure has never precisely matched that of the rest of Britain. That is one reason why it was possible for the system of smallholder farming to continue for so long and why, over the centuries, the Jersey country dweller's character has tended to differ from that of his English counterpart.

Jersey has not known a time when a few families, inheritors of great estates, could wield almost complete power over mere serfs. Nobody, for example, has ever enjoyed enough uncontested influence to wrest land from others by means of threat, dishonest promise or doubtful law. Through time it became a part of the smallholder's perception of things that he was a free man, that none would willingly sell his own small heritage to another and would resist any attempt to force him to do so. Together, they also wielded enough influence over Island government to prevent such a situation arising in law.

In a community where people tended to be judged rather more on what was visible – namely the land they owned and the house they lived in – than on the money they had secretly stashed away, to sell would have been like parting at one and the same time with status, security and, it goes almost without saying, even one's livelihood. Thus if one man, hoping to increase his holding, wanted to buy land from his neighbour situated conveniently close to his own, his chances of success were slim. The soil lay even more deeply embedded in the Jersey smallholder's soul than cupidity in his heart.

As much to the point – there were no peasants in the condescending sense in which the word might have been used in

England, no great chasms of social division, no political tradition whereby the powerful could browbeat the weak. True, the Island had its own hierarchy and was far from being a community of equals. But in the rural areas at least those who were important were not very far removed either in the social order or geographically from those who were not.

Influence in this small, tight community was spread far more evenly than could ever have been found in a nation of many and diverse people. All men had a voice and the population was too small for it not to be heard. While some enjoyed considerable authority and required respect, few of those who had it would have thought to step too far out of line.

There formerly existed in such isolated communities as that in Jersey a strange kind of brake which discouraged individual excesses of any kind. Each had a place fixed by society itself. Any attempt to move from it by bettering one's position (other, perhaps, than by marrying into the right family) would meet with sniffs of disapproval or outright challenge. It is difficult to understand such a situation now. But the consequence of living as one member of a small, distinct and unwarlike group must always be an inclination towards uniformity, a kind of togetherness even where there is hatred. Individuals are cemented together, willingly or otherwise and no matter what their position, by a web of oral history and tradition. It manifests and maintains itself through gossip, by shared experience and the simple fact that through generations of inter-marriage everybody knows everybody else's affairs. The very foundations of Island life ensured the steady presence of a levelling influence. It led to a restraint not just on change of any kind but also on what were judged to be extremes of personal ambition.

Whatever other reasons there may have been, from medieval times onwards there was precious little opportunity for any but a very few to acquire a great stock of land, that most precious Jersey commodity of all, as had been the case in England at the time of the Enclosures. And death and the division of his estate usually put an end to any hopes an individual may have had in life of passing on his wealth entire to others.

Integrated, lacking the sophistication that may be found in

cities, developed by the flow of history in its own essentially rural way, the separate layers of Jersey's social sandwich were therefore less easily distinguished one from the other than would have been the case in England.

*   *   *

At the top were the seigneurs. The office of seigneur now has little significance, if any. But at one time they were, quite literally, *la noblesse*, the cream of local society from whom came many of the notables of the Island, including Bailiffs and Jurats. By reason of the greater income their families enjoyed they were often men of good education and through their position held considerable power in an Island which was insulated from the much greater powers beyond their shores. They were to be treated with esteem although not deference by the ordinary citizen, who anyway was very probably a blood relation through one link or another.

The office of seigneur is an ancient one. Originally it was similar in some respects – although, as it were, on a smaller scale – to that of an English knight enjoying the benefits derived from his sworn duty to the king. In a sense, though, seigneurs in later times could be better likened to chieftains. Within the boundaries of their territories – their fiefs – they had considerable authority. They required a degree of personal allegiance from their tenants (that is, those with holdings in their fiefs rather than renters of land owned by the seigneur, as the title might imply in English).

They also demanded those feudal privileges and dues in labour and kind that came to them by ancient rights through successive generations and from which, directly or otherwise, they obtained a part of their incomes. Both dues and privileges varied somewhat between one fief and another. For example, many enjoyed a right to own a rabbit warren or a *colombier* (a pigeon loft) whose inhabitants, free to fatten on the hapless tenants' crops, formed a valuable part of the manorial diet. Some owned a mill where their tenants would have to take their corn to be ground and who in turn had to help to keep it in repair by providing materials and labour. Some required from their tenants help at

'Some seigneurs owned a mill.'

harvest time or the provision of loads of *vraic* (seaweed) to be put on their land. A few, seigneurs of *fiefs nobles*, even had a right to maintain gallows – although only the Royal Court had the right to condemn malefactors to hang from them.

It is hardly likely that tenants felt any peculiar sense of loyalty to their seigneurs. Some individuals were good; some were bad. They were a part of the fabric of the Island. Probably most people realised that in terms of good government within their own small domains they had an important role to play, somewhat as Connétables have now in running parish affairs.

(Interesting though they are, the scope of this book makes it impossible to provide explanations of such ancient offices as Bailiff, Jurat, Connétable, Centenier, etc. which are unique to the Channel Islands. But details can be found in other reference books.)

Each seigneur had a right, and perhaps a duty, to hold manorial courts where various matters, mostly of a civil nature and including minor disputes, could be settled. Although important cases came before the Royal Court, quite substantial justice based on Norman customary law was sometimes handed out at these seigneurial courts, frequently through a jury of tenants. Thus in a way these were people's courts, intimate and far removed from the paraphernalia, the immense cost and the distant formality which marks justice today. Nevertheless, the judgments must usually have been fair in a rough and ready way simply because those involved almost certainly had an intimate knowledge of the factors behind each case.

The relevance here of the position the seigneurs enjoyed lies in the fact that it was the title they held, their authority and their privileges, which ensured a seigneur's social standing; rather, as might have been the case in England, than the extent of his estate, which could in some cases have been no greater than that of his neighbour.

The fiefs over which each had control varied in size, and the degree of status they conferred on the seigneur tended to vary accordingly. Some of them had names which ring delightfully to the modern ear and provide further proof of Jersey's historical links with Normandy. There were, for example – and still are – the fiefs *du Prieur de l'Islet; des Vingt Livres; de Franche Mauv-*

ellerie; de Crapedoit; de Gondbrette; de Ganouaire; de Robelinoys; de Vaugulême. These fiefs, although of course not the land within their boundaries that did not form a part of the seigneurie itself, could also change hands – perhaps through sale or by inheritance – so that one man could be seigneur of several.

There were in fact a surprising number of seigneurs. One authority has estimated that in the early 1600s there were between a hundred and a hundred and thirty of them – probably one to every fief. Even in the 1950s, when such things were listed, a total of 116 fiefs were noted in the *Jersey Evening Post Almanac*.

Not surprisingly, the high standing in society of so many seigneurs in so small a place tended in former times to make them arrogant, quarrelsome in the usual manner of the Tudor and Stuart periods and, of course, immensely jealous of each other, often disputing before the Royal Court over petty issues in an effort to outrank a rival. An Englishman of good breeding would probably have dismissed most of them merely as oafs and popinjays speaking a barbarous language. That was certainly not how they were regarded by the Island community.

Indeed, for centuries they were an essential part of Jersey society. Apart from dispensing justice within their fiefs and providing many of the Island government's leaders, their presence throughout the community ensured a remarkably democratic diffusion of influence and authority that would not have been found in the United Kingdom. Social restraints meant that few were evil, and many no doubt were good. They set standards. They made it possible for civil affairs to run smoothly and with the least interference from an excessively powerful central establishment, and together they formed an educated élite which was invaluable culturally. One might go so far as to suggest that the true worth of the seigneurial system as it once existed has never been fully recognised. But by the start of the Industrial Revolution the seigneurs' authority and influence, like feudalism itself, was beginning to wane, and with it the power to impose their authority or to benefit from the dues which once went with an important position that was bought or inherited rather than being conferred by Crown, government or vote.

However, the last of these rights was not done away with

until 1966. It enabled a seigneur to claim, for a year and a day, the enjoyment of the income derived from the property of any tenant in his fief who died without direct heirs. By its nature, it seems an excellent example to indicate the variety of sometimes unusual benefits seigneurs formerly enjoyed.

*   *   *

At the bottom of the social sandwich, of course, there came the poor – the landless, the afflicted, the orphan; the hopeless, hapless people to be found everywhere in all ages. The Rev Peter Heylin, who in the early 1600s had referred to the peasants as 'marrying within themselves like conies in a burrow', was the first person known to have published a book about the Channel Islands. He found Jersey 'exceedingly pleasant and delightsome'. But he was shocked by 'children who were continually craving alms of every stranger'.

Pauperism was probably the most serious internal problem the Island authorities had to contend with at that extended time in history when a social conscience, even in the Church, was not so tender, compassionate and all-embracing a thing as it is now. The individual, or his family, was expected to look after himself. It was not the duty of society to do so except in an extreme, and then only grudgingly lest the poor began to take advantage perhaps not so much of public generosity as of the wealth of the individual who had to provide it.

Not surprisingly, such a philosophy meant that try as the authorities might, the pauper remained among them. A year after Heylin's book was published an Act of the States ordained that children of the poor should be taken on as apprentices in order to learn a trade, while those too old or too young to work were to be maintained by businessmen who could afford to do so. The aim was good; the results evidently not so, for the regulations had to be re-enacted time after time in later years. Then in 1666 the Governor, General Morgan, devised what he must have supposed was a good idea. He sought the support of the States for a scheme to send Jersey's paupers, willy nilly, to the young British dominions of Ireland, New Jersey or New England, there to make new lives for themselves. He probably reasoned that because the Civil War had left the Island in such a bad state economically, it would be better, or at least more convenient, to export the problem than to deal with it.

The States – of which the twelve Rectors of the Island's parish churches formed a part – agreed 'in all sincerity of heart, and motivated solely by compassion'. But the United Kingdom authorities did not and the plan was dropped. Later, the States passed another Act forbidding the Rectors themselves to marry 'persons of the lower orders' unless the couple could prove that they were able to support a family.

And so it went on, with various attempts being made to deal with the effects of poverty although never the cause. For example, in 1768 one of the first acts of the newly-formed Jersey Chamber of Commerce was to buy and import some forty tons of barley to be used for the relief of the poor. Perhaps members really were motivated by a growing spirit of charity. More likely, since they had to pay for the cargo, by fear that the simmering discontent which was finally to explode into bloody revolution thirty years later might spread from nearby France to Jersey. Either way it is interesting to note that it was private enterprise rather than government which took action, and then only to mitigate a problem rather than to deal with it.

*   *   *

Rebellion of a kind did, in fact, occur the following year. The spark was a rumour that locally-grown corn was being exported, so encouraging artificially high bread prices. True or false, the news led to men from the northern parishes, including three hundred from Trinity, going on the march to force changes. Very quickly the demands grew to include not only a reduction in corn prices but also the abolition of certain tithes due respectively to the seigneurs and the Church. By the time an angry mob got to the Royal Square a great many others had joined the original protesters. Together they stormed the Court House where, the *Assise d'Héritage* being held, the seigneurs were renewing their oaths of allegiance to the Crown. In the *mêlée* which followed the poor usher was thrown over the railings and what would now be called offensive weapons were brandished. The disturbances continued for five hours. Although no blood was spilt one man present said later: 'I did not believe that any of the magistrates (Jurats) would escape with their lives.' Needless to say, the people's demands were met.

As late as 1847 – during the dreadful period of the 'Hungry Forties' caused by the appearance in Europe (including Jersey) of potato blight – there was another revolt over bread prices. A labourer's wage, fixed at two shillings a day, was not enough to maintain a family. Action was taken by clearly desperate men and women. The rudders of grain ships were removed to stop them sailing (but were afterwards replaced). Then a large crowd, gathering in numbers all the way, marched to Grands Vaux in St Helier. There, despite the efforts of a brave Centenier, they broke into the Town Mills, loaded carts with sacks of flour and started to make off with them. The disturbance ended when the Connétable of St Helier, showing remarkable courage, jumped on a loaded cart and challenged anyone to move it. Nobody did.

Soldiers from the British garrison stationed at Fort Regent later marched in and recaptured the other cart. But the protest was successful. The States agreed to sell bread at below cost, the country Connétables agreed to be more generous in providing parish relief – and rich residents, evidently scared by the possibility of real violence, subscribed the astonishing sum of over £700 to a relief fund.

* * *

Between those with status and plenty and those with neither there remained what can only be described as the middle class. It is a classification fairly new in concept and even now difficult to define. The English middle class began to appear, and be recognised as such, only at about the time of the Industrial Revolution when more and more people enjoyed better incomes and better education and could wield greater influence over all aspects of social affairs.

So far as Jersey was concerned, this indefinite 'middle class' might be said to have included such tradesmen as merchants and shopkeepers, and those involved in building and maintaining Jersey's great maritime fleet of wooden ships. But the greater proportion were most likely the smallholders – the landed proprietors – and their families. Right through to the start of the First World War the latter probably formed by far the most significant part of the total social sandwich. As the prosperity of farming increased thanks to cider, cattle and potatoes, so too did their dominance in Island affairs.

*   *   *

Thus, by virtues of its composition and nature, Jersey's society consisted in the main of men and women who enjoyed a sense of cautious equality between neighbours that would probably not have been found in England, and certainly not after the upheavals of the Industrial Revolution and the growth of that middle class which tended to form a sharp division between the poor and the rich.

There can be no doubt, too, that for the reasons already explored briefly the Island natives had characteristics unique to themselves and which in a number of respects were notably different even from those in the sister island of Guernsey. They knew themselves to be a quite separate people but yet were in part English, even though their history was not of England. In part they were Normans, although for many generations Normandy, as a region of France, had been enemy territory.

Jersey's limited right to self-government, the absence of overlords and the remarkable numbers of men and women who, these days, would be termed self-employed tended to make the Island's inhabitants of former times downright independent, parsimonious and disputatious. They worked hard because they did so for themselves. Despite restrictions on voting rights they enjoyed a strong sense of democracy because it has always existed. They were canny and Calvinistic in a way that often failed to prevent a liking for drink. They were clannish and suspicious of strangers – dour, even. They tended to have a love of money. They were obstinate but at the same time were adaptable, industrious and commercially acute.

However, when it finally comes to an attempt to pinpoint more precisely what even now, when almost too much has changed, are so often referred to as 'the Jersey character' and 'the Jersey way of life', one is left with a feeling of grasping at shadowy shapes glimpsed dimly in the darkness of the past rather than observed clear-cut in the light of the present moment. What definite shapes there are could perhaps have best been noted among the members of the farming community as it once was. After all, in the main they had ancestors of Jersey birth stretching back through the generations. But most have gone now. The Island has altered its course, although that is not to say that the spirit of Jersey has been lost.

Perhaps in the end it must be left to the individual to assess exactly what it is the Island has inherited from the ghosts of its past that still exists within the present generation to make of them an Island community that is different and, in many ways, unique.

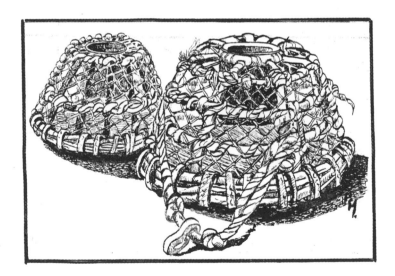

PART TWO

The Land,
the Parsnip and
la Grand' Tchéthue

5.
Jersey's heritage: invisible, ignored

PERHAPS IT WAS the great changes which swept through Jersey, as elsewhere, in the decades after the war that finally encouraged people to look back with an upsurge of almost militant wistfulness on a remembered past – based though it may have been more on sentiment than reality. Whatever the reason, from the 1970s an increasing desire grew to a ragged kind of determination to preserve what was called the Island's 'heritage', which, it was feared, was at risk.

Heritage is a conveniently catch-all word elastic in its use according to personal whim or current fashion. So far as most Island residents have been concerned, it more often applied to certain visual aspects of urban Jersey – old buildings or specific areas – or to keeping the appearance of the coastline and beaches and the countryside safe from violent change. Yet above and beyond such admittted treasures there exists, always unrecognised although never invisible, the land itself. Perhaps of all the assets the people of Jersey have inherited, the greatest is the fertility of the Island's arable soil. It comes not as an unsought blessing from nature but as a bequest passed on by layer upon layer of past generations of Island farmers. In that sense alone it could be said to deserve the same degree of respect and active preservation as even the oldest of man-made monuments to human activity.

People claim from time to time that Jersey has a fertile soil. If that is so, it is the result of the unremitting toil, of a respect for the land and of the good farming practices of centuries of smallholder farming. It is true that the land, like the climate, is generally kindly. It lacks the sticky clay and the plagues of large stones to be found in some places, or the great quantities of hun-

64

gry sand to be found in others. In most areas it is fairly level and easy to cultivate. It is deep enough and it lies over free-draining subsoils. But naturally fertile it is not. It has neither a store of minerals to be released slowly from the mother rock nor a peaty base to provide organic matter, both of which are essential elements if plants are to thrive. On the other hand, it has been said often enough that of all the ingredients that can go on the land to make it fertile the best is the farmer's foot. The tiny fields which once constituted the minute kingdom of the individual smallholder had that in plenty.

There has already been a brief outline of how smallholder farming developed and remained for so long after it had disappeared elsewhere in Britain. There is no point in repeating the details here. It is enough to say that it was the land and what it could provide that counted above all else. Of course, snobbery and a desire to place oneself a rung higher on the social ladder was to be found just as strongly in Jersey as anywhere else. But tradition, the nature of the countryman, the brake imposed by social attitudes on individuals with grandiose ideas, a kind of careful meanness and the laws on inheritance which made impossible the permanent creation of great estates, all conspired to discourage investment in outward shows of wealth.

The Jersey farmer's thoughts were fixed firmly on his land, his crops and his stock. He could be wealthy, and recognised as rich, by such simple things rather than by means of expensive clothes or fine words or delicacy of manners or decorative *fol de rols*. He was wedded to – his detractors might say enslaved by – the principle of a self-sufficiency that is derived from the land. It was a philosophy rooted deep in the mind. It was echoed in the 1970s by somebody who, standing in his one tiny patch of land, and that of little commercial value, was nevertheless able to say in Jersey Norman-French and with obvious contentment: *Quand j'sis ichan, j'sis siez me* – ('When I am here I am at home').

It must be less easy than it once was to understand that simple attitude now in an age so far removed from the soil and so entirely enmeshed in the marvels of technology and the engines of a cash economy and international consumerism that, were any of these to falter, society itself would be at risk of foundering.

*   *   *

The increasing desire to preserve a people's heritage has run in the latter part of this century like a twin alongside an equal desire on a world scale to conserve natural things. The Brazilian rain forest with all its diversity of plant and animal life has been frequently singled out for the closest attention. Strangely, it may seem, the need to conserve the equally vital and just as richly diverse flora and fauna of the living soil on which, like every other human being, the activists themselves ultimately depend for their daily food, has never aroused the same kind of protective enthusiasm – perhaps because they are invisible, unattractive, ordinary and so close as to be literally underfoot.

The Jersey farmer, as with the rest of his kind, knew all about his own form of heritage and conservation instinctively and from centuries of practical experience. Even if he had no clear understanding of biology and organic chemistry, of the unending interplay, the life-and-death struggle to exist, between worms and bugs and crawly things and literally uncountable numbers of microbes and the multitude of different fungi which in balance create a fertile soil, he knew with the same certainty that a fledgling knows it will fly that the land had to be fed. If it was not, hard experience was quick to remind him. Fertility diminished and with it his chances of living well off the one natural resource he owned. There was no call for intellectuals or experts to lecture him on a subject of which he was the master. It was this awareness, coupled with an absence of large markets and the need to maintain themselves and their families as far as possible from a small area of land, which originally led in Jersey to a system of balanced agriculture rather than to a dangerous specialisation in one particular crop or one kind of animal.

Each smallholder grew corn to make the family's bread. Each kept livestock and grew the food needed. Each had a pig or two in the sty and a few fowls running loose and scratching small livings for themselves. And back into the earth went everything the earth had produced. It was an endless cycle in which the manure-heap was the visible element. On to it went the dung- and urine-soiled straw from the corn he had grown and which had been used to bed his livestock. On to it went his own ordure, and almost certainly dead chickens or piglets or even calves which had died.

And where better to dispose of the kitchen waste or the afterbirth from a calved cow? What town dwellers might have seen as revolting material was a matter of satisfaction to a farmer who stood on his gently steaming manure heap in the late autumn forking the rich, rotting and strangely sweet-smelling material on to the cart as the horse dozed while waiting to haul the next load to the field. Back it all went on the land which, in pure sentiment, one might say had given it birth.

In later years large tanks were built beneath the manure pits on larger farms and the seepage from the heap flowed into it, together with the urine from the horse and cow stables. This, too, went on the fields, raised by hand pump and human muscle to large barrels placed on carts. Rich in nitrogen, the liquid manure was sprayed on to grassland. Nothing of it was lost.

Some of the pasture was permanent and was used for grazing or for making hay – for example in the meadows of the valley bottoms or in the apple orchards which slowly came to take up so much land as cider-making became an increasingly profitable industry. The rest of the grassland would be ploughed from time to time and that, like dung, played its part in enriching the land, as did stubble from corn fields and the tops of vegetable crops which were useless for animal feed. All was returned to the precious earth where, in a process of decomposition as biologically complex as would be found in some distant rain forest, it played its part in enriching the land.

There can be few who are totally ignorant about the practical aspects of growing things. But even those few can hardly fail to know the value of organic matter in creating a fertile soil; or to admire the neatness of this kind of perpetual motion. It could be repeated from generation to generation, century upon century. Its by-products were, in truth, the very meat and vegetable matter on which men depended for their existence. And they, too, were transformed and were returned from whence they came. So by invisible degrees what had been Jersey's ordinary soil grew increasingly fertile, far more so than land on the much larger and less intensively worked English farms could ever have been. Only the human corpse escaped from this endlessly sustainable cycle. It, as well, was returned to the land; but in selected places with formality and lament.

* * *

67

There was another natural product which played a vital part in making Jersey's soil productive. Seaweed – *vraic* – is still a valuable harvest gained from the shores. But for centuries demand for one particular kind was so great that controls over its harvesting were necessary to prevent arguments. Even the States regarded it as being so important a product that as far back as 1608 – and on several subsequent occasions – it was ordered that no man should knit the woollen goods, which had by then become the Island inhabitants' chief money earner, during harvest time or the cutting of *vraic* 'on pain of imprisonment in the castle' (Mont Orgueil, where prisoners were housed) on a diet of bread and water.

Vraic provided three quite different benefits. Spread on the land – more usually on grass or on the lighter soils – it was an excellent natural fertiliser. But it could also be dried and was used in a great many homes as a fuel for the kitchen fire, much as peat was used elsewhere. The fire was never allowed to go out and even as late as the mid-1800s visitors could remark upon the 'white smoke issuing perpetually from the chimneys.' The smell was said to be quite pleasant but was not to be compared with the sweetness of smoke from a wood fire.

On an island where family labour was largely unpaid and freely available and where the countryside was so heavily cultivated and lacked woodland, *vraic* as a fuel had the advantage of being free for the taking and saved the expense of buying coal. The alternatives were dried gorse (whose fierce, smoke-free burning was excellent for heating the bread ovens to be found on most of the larger farms) or cuttings from the hedgerows and, later, the apple orchards. The *vraic* fires were probably smouldering things as a peat fire might be rather than flame-leaping and welcoming, but they provided enough heat for cooking with some left over to warm a cold body on a bitter day.

However, it was not merely heat the burning material had to offer. The ash was long recognised as being invaluable as a fertiliser and was carefully hoarded to be returned to the land. While stable manure was fairly rich in the nitrogen on which plants depend for growth, the *vraic* ash was rich in the equally important plant food, potash, as well as other essential minerals including some phosphate. It therefore played its own useful part in maintaining the productivity of the precious soil and was claimed to be especially effective when used on land to be sown with corn. So great was the demand for the ash that it is said a few poor people along the Island's west and south coasts made what must have been a precarious living by gathering the seaweed from the beach, burning it and selling the grey, dusty ash.

There are three distinct kinds of *vraic*. The green 'lettuce' material to be found sometimes in fair quantities in such areas as St Aubin's Bay has never been regarded as being of much use for anything. Another is the laminaria with long, brown ribbon-like fronds. Anchored only loosely to the rocks on the sea bed, it is often torn free by rough seas. It can be seen washed up, sometimes in great quantities, on certain beaches, particularly the long sweep of St Ouen's Bay. Left alone, it rapidly deteriorates into a stinking, slimy, maggot-crawling mess. But gathered fresh, spread on the land and either ploughed in shortly afterwards or left to rot, it is an excellent provider of organic matter.

But at one time the most prized *vraic* of all was the more solid bladder-wrack. Being anchored tight to inshore rocks it rarely came ashore in great quantities as a natural bounty on stormy days. It had to be harvested as might a crop from a field. So keen was the competition to get supplies of this type of *vraic* that the periods of harvesting were fixed by the States as far back as the 1600s. Originally there were three short seasons but the last, in the autumn, was later abandoned because it restricted new growth. Harvesting, usually from March 10 and from July 20, lasted only for some ten days

These brief periods away from the land and livestock and among friends and neighbours became traditionally a kind of party time, perhaps rather as fairs were in England. Whole families followed the falling tide, gathering in what bladder-wrack they could and carrying it as best they were able above the high tide level as the sea rose again. It was hard labour of the hardest, wettest and slimiest kind but, providing there were no arguments about ownership of the precious piles of material, it provided one of the rare opportunities for country people of all ages to get together on a serious pretext but also to have a good time.

Much is made in these more genteel days of the traditional

'...traditionally a kind of party time.'

galettes à vrai, really nothing more than large buns containing currants said to have been baked especially for the *vraicers*. More important, no doubt, were the hot drinks, jars of cider and maybe even calvados and rum which might have been available for increasingly moist and possibly boisterous workers. Some of the *vraic* was hauled into convenient spots for later removal using huge, long-handled rakes. Many gatherers would have been able to take their carts along convenient tracks hacked out of the rocks, a number of which are used by *vraicers* even now.

Many others actually went to sea. They rowed out – men, women and probably children, and perhaps even a little uncertainly if they had been too early at the drink – in boats armed with small curved sickles like those used for reaping at the corn harvest. Leaning over the sides they slashed at the weed clinging to the rocks and brought it aboard, returning when the craft was at risk of sinking from the weight of its load. Such dedication – and it must have required that to gather what could only have been quite small cargoes of cold, wet seaweed in this manner – helps to emphasise the value that was once placed on this material, or the need for it particularly as a fuel.

These days it is only the laminaria that has been washed up which is harvested from the beaches and taken away to be spread directly on the fields, and that to nothing like the extent it might. Most regard it as merely a nuisance. But well into the 1950s, along St Ouen's Bay in particular, there were still a few *vraicers* with their horses and carts. By then more often tractors and lorries were used, although the material was still being loaded by hand. One could also see *vraic* either spread to dry on flat, gravelly patches by the side of the road or, once dried, built into small stacks of dark, crinkly material. These were later sold by auction, not for burning as would once have been the case but usually to farmers with steep côtils which could not be reached by carts loaded with wet *vraic*.

The amount of the material removed from the Island's beaches annually was astonishing. Ansted, a serious and dependable author, suggested in 1893 that upwards of 30,000 loads of vraic were then being harvested every year. Presumably this was the laminaria that is used on the land. Given a fifteen hundredweight load, a good weight for a horse to drag up long and quite steep hills such as those which lead from St Ouen's Bay and leave it lathered at the top, that amounts to something like 22,000 tons of seaweed gathered from the beaches and either burned or spread on Island fields every year. Even if Ansted was a little ambitious in his estimate, a prodigious quantity was certainly once used by the farming community.

But even more to the point, perhaps, is the fact that despite the time and labour involved in taking a horse and cart to the beach, making a load, returning to the farm and spreading the *vraic*, the job was never for one moment considered to be other than worth while. Between them and over many generations stable manure, *vraic*, the smallholder's foot – and an innate sense of good husbandry – worked together to ensure the fertility of the Island's amenable soil.

The richness of Jersey's farmland is, indeed, an inheritance. It remains to be seen whether the same efforts will be made to preserve it in the future as are being made now to preserve other aspects of Jersey's heritage.

6.
The vital rôle of
the simple parsnip

VARIOUS PEOPLE in the past who wrote about Jersey took pains to mention the gardens. They were seen as a feature of many country properties, even the smaller ones. Evidently well tended, they carried a profusion of flowers, shrubs and fruit trees in surprising variety.

Henry Inglis remarked in 1835: 'It is seldom – I might say never – that one sees a house or cottage that is unaccompanied by less or more garden.' Twenty-five years before him, John Stead, always enthusiastic, wrote in his *A Picture of Jersey*: 'Much Pains are taken by all Classes of the Inhabitants to excel in the Quantity and Quality of the Fruits produced in their well-walled Gardens. The flavour and size of their Peaches, Nectarines, Apricots, Plums, Grapes and Pears are not to be excelled in any Country in Europe.' Another referred to the fact that many houses had grape vines growing on their walls. Others mentioned melons, strawberries, raspberries, figs, medlars and even lemons and oranges – the last being usually 'small and so bitter as to be fit only for making marmalade'.

As far back as 1790 a resident in St Aubin was advertising fruit trees for sale, the list including peaches and apricots, many kinds of apples and nearly thirty different varieties of pear, which were once very much favoured as a dessert fruit. Among them, the Chaumontel was especially delicious and sought after. The best weighed a pound or more. Like others, Stead remarked on them and said that they could be sold for £5a hundred, or for as much as 2s.6d. each if they could be got to Covent Garden in prime condition – and that in the early 1800s.

No doubt some of the many seigneurs, determined to maintain their individual place in society, were at one time foremost among those who saw fine gardens and a great variety of produce for their tables as a means of doing so. They were joined later by Jerseymen with large houses and money to spare who had made their fortunes from the sea either through honest commerce, privateering or smuggling. Later still came the growing number of wealthy Englishmen who opted to settle in Jersey. A love of gardens and gardening remains a feature of the Island.

But for the smallholder, as for those seigneurs whose livelihoods often depended more on the produce of their fields than from the dues obtained from the fief's 'tenants', it was the arable land they owned which demanded their unceasing devotion. Apart from what they could harvest from the sea, it was their only natural resource; and, unlike the sea, it was theirs. Apart from human and animal muscle it was all they had. One way or another it could provide almost all the needs of that majority of Island natives who lived simple lives.

James Playfair, the chaplain to an English regiment stationed in Jersey, wrote to his parents in 1781 when agriculture in England was coming to be affected by the Industrial Revolution and the Acts of Enclosure. He remarked disparagingly: 'There is nothing of what may be called agriculture here. Every man has his few acres which are generally his own (and) he labours them with his own hands....' But despite this dismissal of what, apart from the production of cider for export, was still very much subsistence farming as not being 'agriculture', he added later: '...everybody has but little, yet everybody is above want'.

* * *

Nowhere was the smallholder's devotion to the land more apparent than in the immense pains he took in cultivating his soil. That could be seen most clearly in the trouble he took to grow parsnips. Parsnips may now seem an unusual vegetable to make any kind of fuss about. But before potatoes, turnips, swedes and such innovations as mangolds came to be grown in any great quantity, the frost-hardy parsnip was the major, probably the only,

'...the produce of their well-walled gardens.'

root crop. It was a vitally important source of winter food for humans but especially for livestock. Without the juicy parsnip it would have proved difficult, and perhaps even impossible, to keep farm animals from near starvation during the winter months. It was, therefore, not just a matter of a few but of tons. Great quantities were required for the cattle alone. For example, when there was no other succulent fodder available, cows in milk could be fed up to thirty-five pounds a day. Pigs thrived on parsnips.

Playfair observed that 'the root, I am told, grows to the bulk of a man's thigh'. He went on in his note to his parents to mention one neat, labour-saving idea. 'Having trenched the ground with a spade they (the farmers) sow it with parsnips and beans mixed.' When ripe, the protein-rich beans were harvested and given to pigs (and also formed a valuable part of human diet, as in the traditional Jersey dish of *pais au fou*). Afterwards the cattle were put out to nibble at the green leaves of the parsnip tops, and when they were finished the roots themselves were lifted and fed to the livestock.

The reason for this treble-purpose, labour-saving system of cultivation, and of 'trenching with a spade' might be obvious to any gardener who grows parsnips. With their astonishingly long, tapering roots, to do well they demand a rich soil deeply-dug .

The ordinary ploughs of those times could not be made to go deep enough. So there was no choice. The land had to be dug laboriously and slowly by hand, and it was natural therefore to want to get the most from the effort involved. The Jersey spade – wider and longer than the English sort – was an important tool on all Island farms even into the 1950s, although by then its use was becoming limited. But mention of digging the land is made in several historical records. Back in 1692 Sir Charles de Carteret, as seigneur of St Ouen, became involved in a furious row concerning the many feudal rights he claimed over his tenants. Among those subsequently confirmed by a special commission of inquiry – and immediately bitterly contested in the manner of the times – was the duty of every *cinquantaine*, that is, every fifty households in his fief, to dig one vergée of his land.

The yield of parsnips, put by one writer as being 'upwards of nine tons a vergée', was considerable. But so, too, was the demand for them as human food and animal fodder – and so, therefore, was the need to dig considerable areas of arable land. How much land a man could dig in a day depended, of course, on his enthusiasm and the state of the soil. But it must have taken a great deal of wearisome labour to turn over even one vergée (or 2,150 square yards) 'Jersey fashion' – that is, skimming the weeds off the surface of each spit and placing them in the bottom of the newly-opened trench before the actual digging could begin. (Digging 'English fashion' – *à la franche beque* – without the preliminary of skimming was never countenanced.) It must, therefore, have come as a great relief – to say the least – when 'the big plough' was introduced into Jersey farming in about 1768.

*   *   *

Ploughs had, of course, been in use in the Island for a very long time. Invaluable for working land to be used for a corn crop, they were not designed to turn the soil to the depth that a good crop of parsnips required. By all accounts, on the other hand, the original *grand' tchéthue* was a monster. It was said to be able to turn a slice of soil up to a foot wide and as deep as eighteen inches, although eleven inches was usually considered to have been deep enough. According to one later record, to pull it 'two bullocks and six to eight horses were requisite'. Thus the distance separating the man controlling the leading pair of animals from the man controlling the plough must have been at least fifty feet and possibly sixty feet. How such a team fitted into some of Jersey's small fields, and whether in fact they ever did, is a matter for conjecture.

Later, with improved breeds of draught animals and less ambitious ploughs, the number of horses was reduced to four or at the most six. These impressive teams could still be seen at work in the 1930s, when there were still some sixteen hundred horses on Island farms but only seventy-one tractors. By the start of the Second World War, however, the picture had changed. By then the number of tractors had risen to just under three hundred and these slow, lumbering Fordson or International machines with their cast iron cylinder blocks and their great steel wheels, their plough horses.

Much is made of *la grand' tchéthue* in its original form by those who, in the main, look back on the past with a sentiment innocent of experience. But there were probably fewer of them than one might suppose. Their use must have been limited to the larger fields. And simply because the numbers of both men and animals that were needed made dependence on others inevitable, most were communally owned and used by groups of farmers.

Preparing a field for the big plough and actually ploughing it was a time-consuming business. If the field had been turned from the centre outward to the hedges one year, to keep the land level it had to be ploughed inward from the hedges the next time. In either event the plough had to be brought to the field and the reluctant animals harnessed to it merely in order to open up an initial furrow. That done, the ridge of soil thrown up had to be levelled by man and spade. Only after that had been completed could the task of ploughing begin. It called for the labour of at least four men and very probably more. One, and more likely several, was needed to control teams of animals that were perhaps unused to working together. Another held the plough. Two more were required to dig trenches, one at either end of the field for the plough to drop into at the start of each bout.

These trenches were a very necessary part of the ploughing operation. The design of a big plough was such that it would have had to travel nose down from surface level a fair distance – perhaps twelve feet – before it reached its full depth. That would mean, of course, that unless it could begin work immediately quite a large part of the field at either end would not be properly turned. Consequently the trenches, or slots, were an essential part of the operation.

Once the plough and animals had finally left the field there remained a great deal of labouring still to be done. The open furrows had to be filled in and the soil made level with spades, and the large unploughed area at each headland had to be dug by hand. Neatness was the thing when every square yard counted. Besides, men were judged by the state of their ploughland just as much in Jersey as anywhere else.

Deep ploughing in the old-fashioned way was a hugely labour- and time-consuming business, but that did not matter. It was a great deal faster and less laborious – and perhaps more sociable since so many neighbours were involved – than digging with a spade. The other advantage was that, together with a system of crop rotations and the abundant use of stable manure and *vraic*, cultivating the land so deeply also ensured a more generally amenable and fertile soil and consequently higher yields from all that was produced on Island farms.

This fertility was remarked upon by several people who wrote about the Island. Way back in 1835 – well before artificial fertilisers came into use – Henry Inglis took the trouble to make various comparisons of yields (in acres). He reported that the hay, at one ton an acre, was 'a very considerable produce'. He calculated that the yield from an acre of wheat in Jersey was 2,181lb an acre, whereas in the Isle of Wight it was 1,486lb; and while the yield of maincrop potatoes in the Isle of Wight was approximately 20,000 lb per acre, in Jersey the average was 29,000 lb. That last figure works out at 5¾ tons a vergée. Sixty years later Ansted put the yield of what he called early potatoes at fourteen tons an acre, or over six tons a vergée. Yields of that order are impressive even in these days of improved potato varieties and the abundant use of chemical fertilisers, although it has to be said that almost certainly the crop was more mature when it was dug than is the case now with the early varieties.

*   *   *

La grand' tchéthue remains a symbol of the old style of Jersey farming, and quite rightly so. To the onlooker a full team of draught animals drawing this great, cumbersome machine sweetly through land seemingly old on one side but sparkling new on the other while gulls wheeled overhead must have been a breathtaking sight. In practical terms, too, the great plough was a technological advance of considerable importance. But like the parsnip it had its day and then was overtaken by events, although not entirely so. The parsnip encouraged the idea of ploughing land deeply, while the deep ploughing *la grand' tchéthue* made possible remains a feature of Island agriculture even though nowadays the implement is attached directly to the tractor and can be operated by one man sitting comfortably in a heated cab. There is no time now to stop briefly by flagons of cider hospitably placed at either end of the field.

Perhaps the business of ploughing and preparing the land in the old, laborious way indicates one of the more important aspects of the smallholder's manner of thinking. He showed a patient, fussy, almost gardener-like determination to get the maximum possible results from his smallholding through what centuries of experience had taught was good husbandry.

PART THREE

Knitting
Cider
Cattle
Potatoes
Tomatoes
Revolution

7.
Next her legs a pair of Jersey hose white

TAKING THE optimistic view, one could easily believe that it has been Jersey's fate to be dogged by good fortune. It lies, waiting to be recognised, in so many aspects of the Island's history. For example, how lucky that it should be a tiny piece of land surrounded by the sea and set where chance put it. Nicely placed so that, although a part of the British Isles – and a fairly independent part at that – it also lies within sight of France. Its position, and history, ensured that it has had close links with both. Geographically, it was formerly conveniently situated as a focal point, what one might call a marine crossroads, for sailing ships and so of commercial activity.

Naturally, therefore, from very early on the Jersey people became a community very much involved with the sea and maritime trade. At first small and probably open-decked vessels enabled this trade to develop between France and England. But then bigger and more seaworthy ships began to voyage to more and more distant places; to the Baltic countries in the north, to Portugal, Spain and Italy in the south, and eventually even from the early 1600s onwards to playing a significant part in exploiting the cod fishing grounds off the coast of faraway Newfoundland, at that time a precisely appropriate name. Cargoes of the dried cod were frequently taken in Island vessels south to the Caribbean and even to South America, bringing back with them such items as baulks of fine West Indian mahogany from which much of the Island's better furniture was made, and timber from which the Jersey vessels were built.

Some Jersey natives were both smallholders and part-time

deep-water sailors. Others remained on the land although, like most inhabitants of small islands, with connections with the seas around them. In the early days, far back, they could have gained little more than a thin living from the crops they grew, the livestock they raised and from inshore fishing. Apart from the sale of dried fish and perhaps of the fish liver oil that was used for domestic lighting there was little if any export industry in the sense in which we know it today. Then, as another stroke of good fortune, along came knitting.

*   *   *

Knitting for export was a more significant turning point in Jersey's affairs than has ever been recognised. It marked the end of a way of life, basic in the extreme, that had existed for centuries. It created new opportunities for people to continue gaining a living from their land but at the same time to improve their lot. How knitting came to be such a major Jersey industry will never be known. It must have been practised domestically in the Island long before Columbus first set sail westward in 1492. It has been suggested that knitting could have been developed into a money-making business in the latter part of the 1500s following the arrival of the Huguenots, those Protestant refugees who fled to neighbouring areas, including Jersey, to escape religious oppression in France. There, the manufacture of intricately patterned stockings was already a speciality.

Whatever the route by which it came to Jersey, knitting proved as close to being the ideal cottage industry as one can get. Unlike weaving, the alternative means of turning yarn into clothing, it needs no complicated, expensive machinery that can be operated by only one person at a time. All that is required is the raw material, a couple of pointed sticks and a pair of hands. Given enough sticks, it can be done by all the members of the family, young and old, at any moment not devoted to growing food or raising a family.

There were several other factors which encouraged the growth of this local industry. Jersey had the benefit foreigners, including the French, did not of sending goods to, and receiving materials from, England duty-free. It was close enough to react to the influence of Southampton, one of the major export centres during the long and profitable era of the British wool trade. It had the handy presence of a maritime fleet in days when carrying goods by sea was more convenient in every way than by roads that were usually fit only for pack animals. Its seamen traders enjoyed generations of commercial experience, and they had close contacts with distant markets made over the years. Add all that together and it becomes a little easier to understand, although not necessarily to explain, how such a minute and otherwise insignificant place became the centre of an activity whose products could eventually be found in many parts of Western Europe and which flourished for an astonishing two hundred and fifty years.

The way in which knitting for export began in Jersey is as uncertain as the way that the name of 'jersey' came to be given to a particular garment. Certainly the Island seems never to have become especially recognised commercially as a centre for producing this close-fitting article of seaman's clothing.

It has been said that the name may have been derived from a way of spinning the woollen yarn that was particular, although perhaps not unique, to the Island. Another, and more likely, explanation is that it came to be generally adopted because among the many men who line-fished for cod in their small dories off the Grand Banks of Newfoundland right from the early part of the seventeenth century, a great number were from Jersey. All of them wore this warm, snug item of clothing knitted to a traditional pattern by their families or often by themselves during the long sea voyages.

But it was stockings, not fishermen's jerseys, that brought in the money to the Island's settled population. Once again the mists of time make the origins of an item of clothing that came to be called stockings a matter for conjecture. Perhaps they were introduced some time in the middle of the 1500s as a result of the obvious disadvantages of wearing what was then a sort of one-piece garment. These were in fact a kind of knickers and stockings combined and were made of a woven blanket-like material for the poorer people and in velvet or some other expensive stuff for the rich.

It is easy enough to imagine that quite apart from their awkwardness, in practical terms the upper part must have worn out far faster than the leg covering, making a whole new garment necessary while part of it was still serviceable. It is also logical to suppose that when the garment came to be divided into breeches of leather or woven material and separate stockings which could be conveniently fashioned to the shape of the human leg, the latter very quickly became popular. However it was, in 1586, Camden, one of those people invaluable to historians in any age, was able to report: 'The women make a very gainful trade by knitting of hose which we call Jersey stokes'.

By then above-the-knee britches and knitted stockings had become fashionable wear among the Tudors, and producing the latter had evidently already grown into a major Island industry. A Jerseyman, Amyas Poulet, was jailer to Mary Queen of Scots while she was in prison. He reported that at her execution in 1587 she wore 'shoes of Spanish leather with the rough side outward, a pair of green silk garters, her nether stocke of worsted coloured watchett clocked with silver and edged on the tops with silver, and next her legs a pair of Jersey hose white'.

By the time of the Scottish queen's beheading, knitting was so profitable a business that everybody in Jersey appears to have been busily at it, even able-bodied men. This apparent excess of enthusiasm for gaining a cash income by manufacturing goods for export began to worry the Island's government to the point at which, in 1608, it ordained that 'during harvest...all persons shall stop making stockings and work on the land on pain of imprisonment and the confiscation of their work'. One reason for this Act – repeated several times l ater – was the obvious fear that people would forsake the land for the needle and not produce enough food for an isolated community whose supply lines might be cut in the event of yet another war with France and so needed to be self-supporting. No doubt an equally practical reason so far as the States was concerned was that the people might not grow and harvest enough corn to pay the tithes – then most usually paid in wheat – due to the Crown, the Church and the seigneurs.

Of course knitting, like most other activities, was forbidden on Sundays although no doubt it was done often enough, but secretly. And one had to be a little wary not only of strict Church law but also of the general moral standards of the times. In 1615 the Royal Court singled out poor Philip Picot and told him sternly that he was not to knit in the company of girls without there being a chaperon present *pour éviter le scandalle qui en advient.*

Despite the various restrictions they imposed, by this time the Island authorities had come to realise that Jersey was on to a nice little earner. It was time to introduce some kind of quality control. In 1607 they declared that any stockings made of the thinner two-ply rather than the three-ply wool were to be confiscated. But it seems to have taken another ten years before inspectors were appointed to make sure the law was obeyed. The regulation concerning the use of three-ply wool shows that these stockings were not gossamer things but tough and practical. They were regarded not so much as accessories as vital items of clothing in the days long before trousers had made an appearance. Further regulations laid it down that they had to be three-quarters of a yard (27 inches) in length. On average, each pair required some 5½ oz. of yarn.

Sold locally to buyers at the Saturday markets in the Royal Square in St Helier, many went (usually via England) to France and, most likely, to the Low Countries. Some were sent to Italy where, it was said in one report, they were preferred to those of silk which tended to shrink in wet weather. Others were exported elsewhere to markets in southern Europe. There is a record of a note by Jersey merchant Philippe Pipon who, in 1693, told his United Kingdom agent that since stockings were not selling well there, the supplies he held should be dyed to suit the trade with Spain. The agent was also instructed to explore the potential of the Lisbon market.

So far as the Jersey producers were concerned there were several enormous advantages in the knitted stocking trade. Their goods were an essentially important product used throughout Western Europe and further afield by men as well as women of nearly all classes. Not one but two at a time were needed. And they had a limited life; sooner or later all stockings wore out and had to be replaced. Even if the price the producer was paid fluctuated from time to time, the demand, therefore, was conveniently continuous. Thus throughout the seventeenth, eighteenth and the first part of the nineteenth centuries the soft click of knitting needles could be heard everywhere in the Island.

* * *

During the earlier part of this long period, and until woven clothing in linen, cotton and other materials came to be produced in increasing amounts, woollen goods – primarily stockings but also including such items as gloves, waistcoats, and quite probably, 'jerseys' – were the Island's chief, and sometimes only, export. For so tiny a community the numbers produced were indeed prodigious.

In 1758 Jean Poingdestre wrote: 'The greater part of the inhabitants are knitters. There are many houses where man, wife and children, beginning at the age of five or six, have no other employment and may be said to make one pair of stockings every week; which must according to my account come to more than 10,000 pairs weekly.' A couple of decades later John Dumaresq put the figure much lower, at 6,000 pairs a week. To put such figures into context, it might help to remember that during much of the long era of the local knitting industry, Jersey's population was estimated to be in the region of 20,000 souls. Apart from their involvement in the sea, growing food for local consumption and running their domestic affairs, the people of the Island were therefore producing – by hand – anything up to one 27-inch, 5½oz woollen stocking per person every week.

By the time the young Victoria was crowned in 1837 the population had risen to over 35,000, although by then the great era of the Jersey stocking industry had just about come to an end. Nevertheless, as late as 1809 John Stead, writing enthusiastically about the country people and their continuing devotion to the knitting needle, was able to say of the stockings they made: 'Few who have experienced the use of them will willingly lay them aside.' The deeply ingrained tradition of taking up the knitting needles at any spare moment was still there twenty-five years later when Henry Inglis remarked: 'I have even seen women on horseback knitting as they rode to market.'

'The greater part of the inhabitants are knitters.'

Initially, anyway, a limited amount of the wool that was needed probably came from the Island's own small flocks of sheep, whose wool must have been used to make coarse garments for the inhabitants long before knitting goods for export became so universally popular. Writing in 1586, Camden noted that many of the animals had four horns. Later it was claimed they had six 'one (on each side) bent towards the nose, another towards the neck and the third standing upright': while not unique to the Island breed – such as it was – it seems that these multi-horned animals may have been seen more frequently in Jersey than elsewhere. Although probably run together as part of a flock, each animal could be easily distinguished by means of the owner's 'copyright' mark on the ear. These marks are still to be found recorded at several parish halls in *livres de bercail*.

The presence of common land and medieval right of *bânon*, which permitted animals to forage freely over unenclosed areas under cultivation from the end of the harvest until the next ploughing season, continued in Jersey until quite late. But as more and more land was enclosed and turned into separate fields, it seems likely that ownership of sheep tended slowly to become restricted to those who had grazing rights on the open commons too poor to cultivate, particularly in the bleaker areas of the parish of St Ouen and the land along the north coast. No doubt they were looked upon more as a convenient means of turning rough pasture into meat and wool than as valuable farmyard animals such as cattle, horses and pigs would have been. Almost certainly they were small, perhaps resembling shaggy-haired goats rather than downy-fleeced sheep. Undernourished, prone to the many parasites and diseases which can affect them and with much of their spare energy devoted to making horn, it must be doubtful if they produced wool in any great quantity. What they did produce was very probably too coarse to be twisted into the fine yarn needed for the stocking trade, although not for the traditional 'jerseys'.

As the demand for wool increased, so it became necessary to ask the English authorities to release duty-free supplies to the Island. By 1624 the States were pleading with Parliament for an increase in the shipments on the grounds that 'more than 1,000 souls have no other means to get their living but by knitting stockings'. In keeping with the times, not all the consignments of wool went directly to those who needed it. In the 1660s there were protests that the then Governor, Sir Thomas Morgan (he who had proposed sending orphan children to Britain's new colonies), was reserving for himself and his family one quarter of the allowance – and then selling it on at his own profit.

The amount of wool imported annually into Jersey at that time was 2,000 tods, or 25 tons (a tod being 28 pounds). As the industry grew, so did the amount required. During the 1700s annual imports of English wool must have been in the order of 4,000 tods, or 50 tons, while Stead, writing in the early 1800s, said that the quantity imported from England was 5,000 tods, or over 62 tons. If the average weight of wool used each year was fifty tons, that would suggest a figure of nearly 6,500 pairs of stockings weighing 5½ oz. a pair being produced each week from the imported English supplies. Add to that the wool which may have come from the local sheep and perhaps from other sources, and it is quite easy to believe that weekly production might have reached the level suggested by Dumaresq, and possibly even that of the almost unbelievable 10,000 pairs mentioned by Poingdestre.

* * *

These 28-pound bales of English wool were hardly likely to have arrived in Jersey as convenient hanks ready for the knitter, at least not until well into the Industrial Revolution when the invention of the 'spinning jenny' (or more properly the spinning engine) made the mass-production of all kinds of yarn possible. While much has been made by various writers about the Jersey knitting industry as such, few mention the equally necessary business of turning a washed fleece into three-ply yarn. Yet that was itself a part of the industry and quite possibly demanded as much labour as the actual making of a stocking. Stead himself refers to the material as having to be 'combed and perfectly dressed'. Almost certainly the raw wool was washed in England before being baled. But having arrived here it had to be carded by hand to bring the fibres into line (and to remove unwanted material), and then spun into yarn.

Historical records relating to Jersey do not seem to throw much light on the practical matter of how this raw wool was turned into knittable thread of a standard quality. A document in the English state papers of 1596 records that 'the spinning of wools are of three sorts – either upon the great wheel which is called woollen yarn, or upon the small wheel which is called Jersey or Guernsey yarn because that manner of spinning was first practised on these isles, or upon the rock which is called worsted' (Worsted being a town in Norfolk where it was first introduced).

For some, carding and spinning may well have been a full-time occupation. But here, as so often happened, the members of the all-powerful States used their authority partly for their own benefit to keep prices down. In the 1620s they decreed that the rate of pay of wool combers and tailors was to be no more than three *sous* a day. In the same period, carpenters were permitted to earn twice that. Anybody demanding more was liable to a quite heavy fine. This was at a time when a wild rabbit cost three *sous* and a pound of butter was ten. Those comparisons may imply starvation wages for the spinners, as it might well have done in some cases. But equally it suggests that the families of these wool combers could quite often depend on having land available to them which would allow them to grow at least some of their own food; or alternatively that this was woman's work which brought her some pin money.

*   *   *

As with everything else, the long era of Jersey's knitting industry was bound to come to an end. There were several factors involved in its slow demise. Very likely one was that the Island's country folk discovered other far more profitable sources of income, partly from making cider for export but principally from the sudden explosion of the cattle export industry in the early 1800s. But perhaps the major reason was the Industrial Revolution. The introduction of machines to take over what before had been done laboriously by hand enabled clothing materials, both woven and knitted, to be produced cheaply and in great quantity.

Moreover, fashions changed. The old style of breeches and

stockings, once worn universally by men, began to be replaced in the latter years of the reign of George III by trousers made from these new mass-produced woven materials. Both more comfortable and more fashionable in the eyes of the people of Regency England, the change to trousers was probably hastened among the upper classes by a desire to follow the style set by the Czar of Russia during his visit to Britain in 1814 when he and the male members of his entourage wore 'cossack trousers'. While no doubt warm and serviceable woollen stockings continued to be worn by many women, so far as men were concerned the use of below-the-knee breeches and long stockings came in the end to be limited to rural males who wore them with leather gaiters and stout boots, to the liveried staff of the wealthy and to those in the garb of ancient tradition. But in all these cases the stockings had for some time most likely been of cotton or other fine material. Thus the day of the twenty-seven-inch, hand-knitted stocking which for some two hundred and fifty years had brought Jersey a useful income, if not wealth, came slowly to an end.

The industry died with neither bang nor whimper. Strangely, as it must surely seem in an era so much concerned with preserving the past, there is little of it left; few specific records, no oral tradition, no tales, no memories handed down from one generation to the next, nothing in the Island's museum. Not even one stocking made during this long period from hand-carded, hand-spun, hand-knitted wool remains in existence to prove that this great local industry had ever existed.

8.
Avoiding tillage as a painful occupation

JERSEY LIES pretty much in the centre of what was perhaps once – and to some extent still is – the greatest cider-making region in Western Europe. To the north it extended in the United Kingdom through Somerset and Devon into Herefordshire, butting on to those drier areas where barley grew well and where, as a result, beer was the universal drink. To the east, the cider apple flourished throughout Normandy. In one direction orchards could be found as far as the Loire, where the grape took over, and in the other to the great corn-growing, beer-drinking regions of northern France and Belgium. Not surprisingly, for perhaps three centuries, and maybe longer, cider was the Islanders' chief beverage. More than that – it provided them with a valuable product for an export industry to England so profitable that for many generations the apple orchard dominated the rural scene.

Jersey was well situated to nudge its way into the developing English cider market. In the first place it got there first. Or so it is claimed, and probably with good reason for there is every likelihood that the cider apple first took root in Normandy, and thus in Jersey, some time before it did in the south-west of England. In the second place, unlike the producers in Normandy and elsewhere, the Jerseyman did not have to pay duty on goods imported into England. In the third place, at that time water was by far the best medium for the transport of heavy, bulky cargoes like barrels of cider. They could be shipped easily from one port to be distributed from another at a time when most English roads were very often little more than rutted tracks quite unsuited for heavily-loaded wagons. Illogical though it may now seem, it was therefore quite often far easier and cheaper to take a cargo by sea to any of England's small south coast harbours, and then by river inland, than to carry the same goods overland from the countryside immediately surrounding them.

Wine made from grapes was the invention of the southern Europeans, while beer made principally from barley was the drink of the more northern races. Where cider fits into this picture is uncertain. Possibly it had as much to do with the climate as with human preferences since generally speaking the apple tree is suited to conditions which do not favour either corn-growing or vineyards.

Shining through the uncertainties about the origins of cider-making in the region is the simple fact that despite the trouble involved in producing them, almost universally people have long preferred alcoholic drinks like cider, beer and wine to plain water as a prime beverage. Before fermented apple juice became popular in Jersey, the drink was either mead – (*baechet* in Jersey Norman-French) – which had been fermented from honey, or *vitou* made, according to one more recent recipe, from honey and water and the addition of ginger and dried elderberry flowers.

It is easy enough to picture the Island as it was before the arrival of the apple tree. Nearly all the primeval forests had long been cut down either for fuel or so that the soil could be cultivated. Its high tableland must have been a bare, windswept place then. Rather as the more desolate parts of Europe still are, much of the vegetation was rank but was nevertheless filled with flowering plants of many kinds. They provided pollen and nectar for innumerable colonies of wild bees. As it still is in many parts of the world, the honey they – and later, hives of more domesticated bees – produced was highly prized in the times long before sugar appeared on the pantry shelf. The *baechet* and *vitou* made from it must have been almost equally valued.

*   *   *

Towards the end of the Middle Ages – say from the 1400s onwards – the Island had come to be marked by small, individual farmsteads. As explained in a previous chapter, the ancient system of strip cultivation of open areas of arable land practised in England for so long by clusters of villagers mutually dependent on each other was already beginning to fall out of favour in Jersey. Instead, each holding (a very appropriate word at that time) had its own small, separately owned cultivated patches producing just enough to satisfy the smallholder's needs. In addition, each smallholder had certain rights to common grazing on land that was not used for growing crops, which is to say the greater part of the Island.

Thus by the time the business of making cider got under way, possibly some time in the 1500s, the Jersey countryside was beginning to take on something of the unique physical appearance it has today – a lack of villages but rather of individual farmsteads; a number of small, enclosed fields; a multitude of winding paths (the *chemins de quatre pieds*), many of which were even then becoming the maze of *chemins de huit pieds* which developed into parish roads where even now it is easy enough to get briefly lost.

The earliest mention of fields or *clos* is said to date as far back as 1395. The word *clos* is still the name generally given to Jersey fields and is usefully descriptive as suggesting a boundaried area. These small patches, originally wrested from the wilderness, needed to be enclosed for two good reasons; the crops growing in them had to be made safe from invasions by livestock grazing on the surrounding common land and at the same time needed shelter from the salt-laden winds that blew from every direction off the sea.

Perhaps there is yet a third reason. It might be found among today's suburban gardens, one fenced off from the other both front and back. Such fences ensure privacy but also suggest that now, as then, there remains a fundamental need among ordinary people to create tiny, recognisable kingdoms, while the gardens themselves reflect just as strong an atavistic desire now, as then, to have some land of one's own in which to grow things.

That simple picture may help to indicate how Jersey probably looked at the time when the first cider apple trees made the short journey across the sea from Normandy and, over the years that followed, dramatically changed the Island's appearance. When apple orchards began to appear is anybody's guess. But with the close links the Island had with Normandy it is almost certain that

95

'The inclosures are planted with apple trees under which cattle feed.'

cider-making developed in Jersey at the same pace that it did there. Equally, a slowly increasing population was one of the factors which meant that there was no longer a surplus of the sweet honey there had once been to be turned into mead. With plenty of land to spare for planting trees, cider was the obvious alternative drink.

In historical terms, events moved swiftly and, relatively speaking, in no time at all Jersey's countryside must have come to be dotted with orchards planted within the shelter of the small fields. At first only enough cider was produced to provide the smallholder and his family with a vital beverage. Then more was made to sell on the home market. Slowly production grew as merchants, perceiving that there existed an untapped market in England, started to exploit a new commercial opportunity. So it was that the smallholder found himself for the first time with a product which came from his own land that was a commercially profitable export commodity.

Cider-making most likely came into existence shortly before the knitting industry did, and continued for some while after the latter had ended. It seems reasonable to suppose that both export trades grew and prospered for the same principal reasons – the existence of a maritime fleet which could provide cheap transport and the fact that no duties had to be paid on goods produced in Jersey and landed in England.

Allied to the ancient lure of the sea, there grew in time such an enthusiasm for making cider and knitted goods for sale overseas at a healthy profit that in the 1680s Jersey diarist Jean Poingdestre complained that 'husbandry was decay'd' and that the people 'avoided tillage as a painful occupation'. Quite apart from their probable truth, the cautionary remarks suggest a sharp division between what the people wanted and what the States considered to be necessary. The quite reasonable wish of the people was to gain a cash income without the sweat and toil that went with cultivating the land. The States, on the other hand, wanted corn – enough both to feed the people without having to upset the Island's balance of payments by importing it and sufficient to pay, in corn, the tithes due to the Crown, the Church and the seigneurs.

There was good reason for the Island government's disquiet.

In the last years of the 1600s, Philippe Falle recalled that in the early part of the century Jersey not only produced enough corn to feed its inhabitants but exported some to St Malo. Now, he said, the people 'must be supplied from England, or in time of peace from Bretagne in France. They have often gone as far as Dantzig in the Baltic, invited there by the cheapness of the market'. Another writer at about this time maintained that Jersey was then growing only half the corn it needed.

By 1673 the area of apple orchards, and the number of new properties being constructed, had increased to the point at which too much arable land really was being taken out of the production of corn. The members of the States, many no doubt themselves cider makers and realising the value of the export trade in cider, nevertheless decided that they had to act. Taking what would appear to be one of the least harmful options, they ordained that no houses were to be built in the countryside unless surrounded by twenty vergées of arable land, the areas around the ports of St Aubin and Gorey being excepted.

In the same decade the States had to deal with other matters of concern. First of all they found it necessary to prohibit the import of cider and cider apples from Normandy. The competition was having a bad effect on the local trade. Moreover, it must have been all too easy to bring both in and then to ship them on to England, claiming them to be the produce of Jersey, so not being required to pay English duties. The ban appears not to have been effective. In 1679 the States went on to petition Charles II directly, complaining that Normandy apples and cider were 'commodities too much abounding and already too much with us'. What seems to have happened is that Sir John Lanier, the newly-appointed Governor, whose activities by reason of his office could not be regulated by the States but only by the Crown, had signed licences allowing two people to import such goods and was prepared to grant more, without doubt at a profit to himself. In doing so he was in fact only following the lead set by the previous Governor in the days when one squeezed every penny one could out of the position one held.

The petition graphically describes the consequences of Lanier's decision. 'Fifty to sixty hogsheads (2,700-3,240 gallons) are landed at a time at the gate of y'r Castle Montorgueil' (to be retailed there and in the neighbourhood). 'Many of us have seen with our own eyes the Castle and the Avenues to it replenished with all sorts and sexes of people drinking even to excess and drunkeness, three or four hundred at once chiefly upon Sundays and during Divine Service.'

Now, three centuries later, it is difficult to understand why there was any need to import Normandy cider unless it was to the Governor's profit. There seems to have been plenty of it produced in Jersey. Writing three years after the States petition had been sent to Charles II, Jean Poingdestre remarked: 'There is hardly a house in the Island, except St Helier, that does not have an orchard of from one to two vergées sufficient to produce twenty hogsheads a year.' Since one hogshead equals fifty-four gallons, that would amount to over one thousand gallons of cider. Poingdestre may have been a little generous in his estimate. Certainly it seems an awful lot for one household's needs. But then perhaps the amount is not so excessive as it may seem. Any ordinary working adult drinking a quite reasonable three pints a day would consume one hundred and thirty-six gallons of liquid a year. Besides, since wine was only drunk by the wealthy and beer had to be imported and paid for, locally-produced and home-made cider was the only sound beverage easily available. And so far as those with land were concerned, in terms of cash it was free and any surplus could be sold easily enough to a merchant.

To juggle with figures a moment longer; if the population of Jersey at that time was about twenty-thousand souls, and supposing that each man, woman and child drank only one pint of cider a day, the local demand for what by then had become the Island's normal beverage could not have been far short of a perhaps surprising one million gallons a year. What is clear is that by the end of the 1600s Jersey had become an island both of knitters and of cider-makers – and drinkers – to the extent that Philippe Falle was able to write in 1692: 'I do not think there is any country in the World that, in the same extent of ground, produces so much cider as Jersey does, not even Normandy itself.'

*   *   *

Besides producing an invaluable cash income for many smallholders, as touched upon earlier, the cider apple was also responsible for a dramatic change in the Island's appearance. Previously, apart from the steep-sided valleys, there could have been little to please the eye of a modern romantic but a sense of exposure and flatness and big East Anglian skies; of small enclosed fields, large expanses of rough common land and a formless pattern of houses held together by a spider's web of roads. As such, it was not suitable terrain for apples. They needed much more shelter than did a crop of barley or wheat or beans or parsnips from the rough winds that could blow unhindered from any direction off the sea. To protect the new apple orchards further, where stone was easily available stout walls were built. More usually high banks were thrown up to strengthen those which had originally been created around the fields. On top of them were frequently planted further windbreaks of trees such as the Jersey elm or impenetrable hawthorn.

Poingdestre wrote: 'About a hundred years since the land lay almost open with few enclosures; but of late people have applied themselves to make fences.' Falle added: 'Not so much fences as in England but great bulwarks of earth sometimes ten feet high with thickness answerable to the height, with a hedge of whitethorn on the top.' The latter grew within a few years 'into a thicke hedge sufficient to prevent any thing from breaking into ye ground within it', which suggests as much a need to keep out a neighbour's animals as to provide shelter from the weather.

Although no longer the 'bulwarks' they once were, these banks remain a delightful feature of the more untouched rural areas of the Island, giving the country roads something of the feeling of paths in a maze.

The apple tree was the cause of another change. As the demand for cider increased, so it became worth the effort to take more and more of what had been uncultivated, unfenced common land and turn it into enclosed orchards. No doubt the job of reclamation entailed a great deal of physical labour, while the actual planting involved almost as much. Thomas Quayle remarked: 'Careful cultivators will take extraordinary pains in digging holes for planting.' They could, he said, be taken to a depth of five feet with 'a layer of green furze laid at the bottom to keep the ground loose and open during the first two years'. With that degree of work involved in the planting, never mind the rest of the labour involved, it cannot be surprising that many of these new enclosures were of a modest size and probably no larger than the original fields surrounding them.

* * *

It might be true to say that the arrival of the apple marked the beginning of the end of that ancient form of agriculture which until then had been based partly on the existence of large areas of open commons where the smallholder's livestock could be grazed under the watchful eye of a child or an old member of the family. As the creation of new orchards and arable fields ate slowly into what had been common land there grew – out of necessity – a system of farming similar to what we know today in which land held in common by a number of individuals no longer played any significant part.

That move away from mutual ownership may seem a small change but was nevertheless socially significant. The pre-medieval system of working arable fields collectively on a village basis was to continue in England until it was done away with at the time of the Industrial Revolution. In Jersey, on the other hand, while relatives and neighbours continued to provide help when it was wanted, by the late 1500s it appears that communal dependence was giving way to a kind of individualism based on the independent farming unit.

Equally significant, although in a quite different way, was the change in the views of those who used the Island's roads. In early May particularly, when the orchards were briefly clothed in faintly perfumed blossom of pink and white, Jersey must have been a place of outstanding beauty to all but those who had a fear of being enclosed in the tunnels of greenery they had to pass through as they walked along the narrow roads.

James Playfair, the English garrison's chaplain in the early 1780s, was one of several at about that time who remarked on the unique appearance of the Jersey countryside. Writing to his parents, he mentions the field banks 'planted thick with trees so that from the roads you can scarcely see thirty yards about you anywhere, and the only view that one can have of the island is from the tops of steeples from which it appears like a forest so that you see nothing but wood'. Much later – in 1858 – Edward Gastineau's guide for tourists mentions the Island's lanes: 'Here you may ramble all day sheltered from the burning sun...the trees overhanging, you have a beautiful canopy of blossoms over your head.' The best time for such a walk, he suggested, was in the fading light of evening (presumable in late summer) when the glow-worms, of which there were then plenty lurking in the high banks, had put on their tiny lights.

Playfair told his parents that 'one fourth of the inclosures are planted with apple trees under which the cows feed.' Thomas Quayle, writing three decades later, confirmed this almost astonishing figure. 'One fourth part of (Jersey's) arable land,' he observed, 'is computed to be occupied by apple trees, most extensively in the parishes of St Martin, Grouville, St Clement and St Saviour.'

Depending on whether the season was good or bad, the average amount of cider Jersey was producing during the latter part of the 1700s and for much of the 1800s was enormous. In 1801 the Rev François Le Couteur (then the Rector of Grouville and delightfully described as 'Rector, Patriot and Expert on Cider') put the annual production at between 1.6 million and 1.8 million gallons, of which about one million gallons were consumed locally. Other records of the period seem to confirm this level of production. One writer suggested that something like five hundred gallons of cider could be produced per vergée. If that is correct one might guess from these figures that there were some 3,200 to 3,600 vergées of apple orchards; but that is no more than a juggling with unconnected and unconfirmed numbers.

* * *

What is sure is that by the start of the nineteenth century the knitting industry, which by then was just beginning to fade away, had already been firmly replaced in terms of profit – through that good fortune which has so often smiled on Jersey – by a very profitable export trade to England in cider. For example, in the five years between 1809 and 1813 an average of not far short of a million gallons a year was being shipped to the United Kingdom.

So great was the interest in cider production, both for personal and local use and for export, that many smallholders with larger areas of land found it worth their while to go to the considerable capital expense of installing an apple crusher and press on their farms, and the building in which to put them.

The crushers were large, circular troughs made from stone taken, so it is said, from the softer and more easily workable granite found in the French Channel Island of Chausey. The apples were put in it and reduced to pulp by a stone wheel fitting in the trough and turned by an amenable horse. Each batch of pulp was then transferred to the press, where it was held in place, square layer upon square layer as in individual parcels, by straw or, later, hessian material. Finally, when a certain height had been reached, boards were placed on top of the heap and the juice extracted by applying pressure to the boards through a massive screwed iron shaft fitted firmly by means of oak beams and iron uprights to the base of the press.

Perhaps it is indicative of the smallholder's character that the manufacture of cider remained on the farm rather than becoming a separate industry. Two factories were established in the early 1800s from which, said Plees, 'the liquor is excellent'. But both failed.

By modern standards there was a deplorable lack of hygiene in making cider, although it seems never to have done any harm except when the drink was taken in excess. And very probably not all that was produced was good. As far back as 1692 Philippe Falle wrote: 'We have (apples) in such plenty that it is not possible that we should be nice in gathering them, and by improving afterwards by Art that sea of liquor that is drawn from them, than are others who have less.' It was the common practice, he added, 'to mingle all, sweet and sour, too often ripe and green confusedly together'. It appears that time did not entirely improve the Art. In 1835, Henry Inglis warned his readers: 'The cider retailed in St Helier is in general detestable.' The reason may well have partly been due to carelessness. But quality also depended on the weather, good or bad, and on the habit of apple trees to bear heavily in one season and badly in the next. Thus some sweet varieties might crop well in any one year, and the sour less well. The art lay to an extent in using the right proportions of both, and with a limited area of orchard the individual smallholder was not always able to make the best mix.

The choice of varieties that was once available was enormous. J.G.Speer, writing on Pommage in the 1970 Bulletin of *La Société Jersiaise*, mentions sixty-five as recorded by historian and dedicated Jerseyman Dr Frank Le Maistre. But as both Dr Le Maistre and Speer have pointed out, there were certainly many more than that which have never been identified. No doubt a good few originated in Normandy. The names (some in Jersey Norman-French) trip as lightly off the tongue as do those of the Island's fiefs – *Musé de Boeu* (bull's muzzle), *Arseul, Amer Doux Blanc* (Amer's sweet white apple), *Le Doux au Vêque* (Vêque's sweet apple), *Pepin La T'nue* (Pepin's seedling), *Noir Binet* (Binet's black apple), *Coccagee*. Each cropped differently, each produced a different liquor and no doubt each had its enthusiasts who could safely be left to argue among themselves on the merits of their favourites.

*　　*　　*

Almost like dissimilar twins, the two industries of knitting and cider-making grew together, and grew old together. The death of the trade in knitted goods preceded that of exporting cider by perhaps sixty years. By the mid-1850s conditions were changing fast. The profits from the cider orchards were proving to be small beer compared with those which could be derived from a cattle export business which had begun to develop with a quite remarkable speed in the early 1800s, and from growing potatoes.

Cider continued to be produced for shipment to England, although by then the volume of exports had fallen dramatically from the halcyon days. They remained steady at about 100,000 to 150,000 gallons a year until about the middle of the 1800s. By the 1860s, though, exports had dropped to 35,000 gallons. In 1874 the quantity was a mere 4,000 gallons and the next year only 2,880 gallons of Jersey cider were shipped to the United Kingdom.

The causes of death were simple. It was not just that Island producers were finding other and more profitable products. One consequence of the Industrial Revolution in England had been the vitally important construction of a system of canals and of improvements to the roads. From the 1830s onwards there was also the almost frantic development of a railway network. Together, they at last made it economically sound to create cider manufactories in such counties as Somerset and Hereford in the knowledge that conditions were now favourable for farmers in the surrounding areas to provide them with the huge quantities of the apples they needed.

Of course, cider-making on a commercial scale had been in existence in this part of the United Kingdom for about as long as it had been in Jersey. In the early 1700s Daniel Defoe was touring in the Honiton and Exeter areas of Devon, and writing in 1725 he noted disapprovingly: 'They tell us they send 50,000 hogsheads of cyder every year to London, and what is still worse, that it is most of it bought there by the merchants to mix with their wines, which if true is not much to the reputation of the London vintners.'

Anyway, by the late 1800s the Jersey farmer who owned his small orchards and made cider on a modest scale, and who was additionally hampered by what were becoming relatively high transport costs, was slowly, and perhaps not unwillingly, edged out of the export business.

Although the production of cider for sale overseas was coming to an end, the orchards were still cropping. For a while great quantities of apples were sent to these new cider factories in England. Between 1854 and 1857, for example, shipments were in the region of 2,800 tons a year. But the last, quite brief, convulsion of the dying export trade came not in the form of the fruit itself, nor of a drink, but as a condiment. For several years from 1880 onward something like 30,000 to 40,000 gallons of vinegar were shipped from Jersey. Almost certainly it was produced from cider. Perhaps it was appropriate that the very bacteria which had once been the bane of the cider-maker's life were responsible for turning the alcohol in it into acetic acid.

Cider production for home consumption still went on in Jersey for perhaps another seventy years, although on a slowly reducing scale. It continued to be a staple drink for many small-holders and others, and making it was very much a part of the tradition of farming life. No Breton gang – on whom the Island farmer once so much depended – who came for the summer season to dig the early potatoes, help with the *branchage* and hay-making, and hoe the young winter crops could be induced to budge without the presence of at least one barrel of cider. However, few if any young trees were planted and the area of cider orchards grew slowly smaller. In 1930 there were 1,740 vergées. By 1939 the area of ageing orchards had dropped to 1,200 vergées. By 1956 there remained only 417 vergées of a crop which had once been claimed to cover a quarter of Jersey's arable land.

Although both thrived independently for perhaps two hun-dred and fifty years, there are unfortunately no reliable records which might give an insight into the kind of profits that could be made either from the sale of knitted goods or of cider. Maybe by the standards of modern economic thinking they were never very great. But the labour was there in plenty; and, as far as cider was concerned, so was the land.

*   *   *

What is clear is that right through the latter part of the 1600s and onwards, as cottage industries both knitting and cider-making were far more attractive commercially to the canny smallholder than, for example, growing corn for sale on the local market as he was so often urged to do. What was of special importance was that between them they provided a means for succeeding generations of Jersey farming families, despite their few vergées of precious land, to move eagerly into the world of cash economics and international trade. They removed (although not entirely) that dependence on mere subsistence farming which was still common in many parts of the United Kingdom right up to the time of the Industrial Revolution.

Knitting needles and apple orchards enabled an ancient

system of farming based on the independent smallholder owning only a little land to absorb the pressures for change from external sources while itself undergoing internal change. And the small-holder himself was able to remain comfortably in business during the time of the Industrial Revolution and afterwards, when agriculture in the rest of the British Isles was enduring an awful period of fundamental transition.

By doing so, they ensured for the smallholder a degree of prosperity during an extended period of history that their counterparts in England never knew; and prepared the ground, as it were, for the years of even greater prosperity derived from the cattle and early potato trades that were to follow.

In that sense alone, sheep's wool and apple juice played a more important part in the development of Jersey's social history than is perhaps generally realised.

9.
This fraudulent importation of cattle from France

GOOD FORTUNE arrives in many disguises, its presence often recognised only long afterwards. In the second half of the 1700s there occurred one of those events which was to change the course of Jersey's agriculture as surely as did the early potato nearly a century later.

For some time the Normandy farmer had been in the habit of shipping his fat cattle to nearby Jersey. There they were grazed for a few weeks before being sent on to England to be sold at the many town fairs and markets held regularly throughout the country. By doing so it could be pretended on import papers that they were Island-bred and thus free from the excise duties imposed on cattle from foreign countries. No doubt some Jerseyman were quite happy with this situation. After all, money was to be made from the rent for grazing if from no other source. But, not surprisingly, people in England began to complain not just of French deviousness but also of the tendency to glut the livestock markets which resulted. However it came about – possibly through pressure being exerted on them by the English authorities – in 1763 the States concluded that something would have to be done. They banned the importation of live animals from Normandy. Although there was a risk of heavy fines, evidently not everybody observed the law. It had to be renewed in 1789, 'the fraudulent importation of cattle from France having become a most alarming matter'.

Once again the States banned the trade, and did so with promises of penalties similar to those threatened the last time. Anybody found landing cattle from France faced the risk of a severe fine, the forfeiture of his boat and equipment and the immediate slaughter of the beast, or beasts, the meat to be distributed to the poor. Apparently this second time around the legislation was effective.

The desire to prevent fraud is one version of the story, and perhaps the most probable. Some aficionados of the Jersey breed have interpreted matters differently. They say that despite the reason given by the States, the ban was actually imposed in order to maintain the purity of the Jersey strain of cattle, in which English farmers were just starting to take a commercial interest. Supporters of either view could present as evidence the fact that Guernsey, too, restricted imports of Normandy cattle; although not until 1824 – thirty-five years after Jersey.

There may have been other factors involved. For example, there could have been a real need to isolate Jersey from certain serious bovine diseases. Among them was what was then called cattle plague but is now known as rinderpest. It had been endemic in Europe for centuries and flared up from time to time. Far worse than foot and mouth disease in its effects, it appeared in the early part of the 1700s and again – perhaps significantly so far as the 1789 ban is concerned – in the last decade of the century. Huge numbers of animals could be infected during these outbreaks. As late as 1865 over a third of a million head of cattle were said to have been affected by the cattle plague in the UK alone. It was not finally eradicated until 1877. Because of the import restrictions, however, Jersey was not affected at any time.

Or again; 1789 was the year which saw the start of the French Revolution. Although enjoying a troubled peace, the British remained suspicious of the French. Those holding great power grew more fearful still when the French peasants began to turn against a dissolute and corrupt monarchy. Just possibly the unrest which was so soon to turn to bloodshed might spread to England. So there were good reasons why Britain should hold France at arm's length even in matters of trade – and particularly since the southern outpost of the British Isles was being improperly used as some kind of tradesman's entrance to the United Kingdom.

Whatever the reason, the effect of the 1789 Act of the States – intentional or otherwise – was to save the Jersey breed of cattle from contamination by outside sources both genetically and in terms of the risk of bovine diseases. Nobody then could possibly have forecast the extraordinary consequences, or the astonishing benefits, the decision was to bring to the Island's smallholders in the decades that followed. As though by the intentions of good fortune, the ban arrived at precisely the right moment in Jersey's history. To understand why this was so it might be worth while to look briefly at the way affairs were developing outside the Island.

Although the Industrial Revolution was responsible for causing misery among untold millions of ordinary people in the United Kingdom, in the longer term it also brought many benefits to the nation as a whole, not least in agriculture. Improvement pervaded the air throughout rural England. Nowhere could it be detected more strongly than in the urge to improve the breeds of every kind of farm animal. Until then poor communications were one reason why Britain – like the rest of Europe – had many regional kinds of cattle. They came in splendid variety. Some were without horns, some had upcurving horns as big as bicycle handlebars. Some were red, some black, some white, some dappled. Some were huge, others tiny. Some gave plenty of milk, others produced plenty of beef. Some were tough and hardy, some were less so. And so it went on. But while the cattle within each region were roughly of a kind, no real effort had ever been made to improve or even fix the better qualities of these walking, breathing, breeding production units, to create some kind of uniformity and to develop them into specific breeds with an increased potential for profit.

Suddenly – at about the time Jersey imposed its ban on cattle imports – there came from several sources, and for good economic reasons, the desire to do so either through selecting the best of the strain, by crossing outside the strain or by breeding within it. Lacking knowledge of genetics, these practical farmers nevertheless made some astonishing changes during the 1800s – not just in creating and fixing a standard of conformation and colour for each breed but more importantly in ensuring dependable fertility and a consistent ability to produce milk, or beef, or both.

That is not to say that in this respect man had been idle

110

during the many centuries before. Take two examples – the Normandy and the Jersey strains. Both had common ancestors and, separated by nothing more than a short stretch of water, both had always existed as neighbours. Yet through centuries of selection, by the start of the 1800s each had become a quite different kind of beast.

With broad green acres of pasture at his disposal, what the Normandy farmer wanted was a big animal, strong enough to pull a plough or haul a cart; something that, in time, could be slaughtered to provide a good carcase of beef; a cow which, additionally, could provide milk for the homestead with enough of the right quality of milk left over to be turned into a saleable product. What he got eventually was a breed of big, beefy cattle whose females weighed in at 12¾ cwt and stood an impressive four-feet-six-inches high at the shoulder. In addition, the cows provided the kind of rich milk from which it was possible to produce what were to become such famous cheeses as Camembert and Neufchatel.

The requirements of the Jersey smallholder, on the other hand, were totally different. He lacked large areas of pasture to support herds of big, fat, slow-maturing cattle. Indeed, until well into the 1950s it was the common practice to limit the amount of grass available to an animal by tethering each one in a herd individually. As soon as the horns were grown enough a chain was put around them to which a rope was attached. In this manner they could be led out to pasture in groups and there tied to long chains attached to iron pegs that were driven into the ground. Having thoroughly eaten a semi-circle of new grass, they would then be moved forward a little. It was a time-consuming task that had to be done two or three times every day. But it did have the advantage of making the most economical use of the limited area of pasture available and, by handling, encouraged the animals to become as docile as domestic pets.

But to return to the needs of the Island's smallholders in former times. Traditionally, beef never did form a great part of the diet of a community where every rural homestead, however small, had a pigsty and a pig or two grunting in it. Jersey was always a place for pork and ham, never barons of beef. James Playfair, writing to his parents eight years before the ban on

'As soon as the horns were grown enough a chain was put around them to which a rope was attached.'

imports was imposed, remarked upon the 'apple trees under which cows feed' and added later of the country people that 'they sometimes feed cattle but their chief animal food is pork'. If the smallholder wanted big draught oxen he could get them from Normandy rather than breeding them himself. (The males must, incidentally, have been emasculated to make them amenable and so could not have been bred from, thus helping to keep the Jersey type of cattle free from contamination by the Normandy type.)

So the pressure of circumstances obliged the Jerseyman to develop a quite different sort of animal from his neighbour across the water. What he wanted was something small, which matured quickly and – because the young males had little market value as beef – females which would live and breed for many years without having to be replaced too often. He wanted a cow which produced large quantities of milk, but not muscle, in relation to the amount of food it ate. He also wanted the kind of beast whose milk contained plenty of fat with those large fat globules which made it easy to turn cream into the best quality butter for sale either locally or in England.

What the Jersey smallholder eventually got, then, was a petite breed in which the cow weighed a mere 7½ cwt. and stood only four feet high at the shoulder. Of little value for draught or as a meat producer, she was to prove the best butter-producing strain of all the dairy breeds in the British Isles or, indeed, anywhere else.

The differences which slowly developed over time between the Jersey dairy variety of cattle and the Normandy dual-purpose variety enabled one to become famous and to travel the world, while the other stayed at home in quiet anonymity.

The quite sudden burst of interest in improving all kinds of farm livestock by thoughtful breeding quickly spread through the British Isles, including Jersey. But unlike others in Britain who could go elsewhere to any strain which might improve their own, farmers in an isolated island made yet more so by the ban on imports of live cattle had to concentrate their efforts on improving the few cattle they had. That, too, proved to be fortunate. By using, out of necessity, the technique of close inbreeding the farmer was probably able to fix, and improve, certain character-

113

istics more quickly than would otherwise have been possible.

In the early part of the nineteenth century the Island type was, in fact, not very much, judging by today's standards. The potential was there but not a lot else. On to the scene steps Jersey Militia Colonel (later Sir) John Le Couteur, of Belle Vue, St Aubin. In his time he was a man of considerable local status and influence, being described as 'soldier, author and agriculturist'. It seems to have been Sir John who took a particular lead in encouraging this new scientific approach to breeding.

At the time of the 1789 ban, Jersey cattle came in a variety of colours from white through to a sort of mulberry black. Worse, though, was their appearance. Sir John described them as 'ungainly, high-boned and ragged in form'. One drawing made some time in the early 1800s shows an extraordinarily ugly animal, long in the leg, a back as lumpy as a mountain range, lacking any sign of a barrel chest and seemingly close to either severe depression or starvation. A second drawing of the 1840s – like some rather overdone 'before and after' comparison – shows 'Beauty', selectively bred by Sir John. She was a quite different beast and seems to have had much of the appearance of the standard type today.

With growing interest in improvement and with evidence of a potential for the sale of Jersey cattle beyond the Island's shores, it may seem a little strange – or scanty historical records have failed to show it was otherwise – that it was not until well into the 1830s that any mutual effort was made by the rural community either to improve the Island breed or agriculture in the general sense. Some farmers finally got together to promote the common good in the autumn of 1833, when what is now the Royal Jersey Agricultural and Horticultural Society was founded. But a further thirty-three years elapsed before the society formed what is still called the Herd Book. One of the responsibilities of the latter was – and remains – to keep a register of cattle as proof of their Jersey origin and so that their ancestry was available for breeding purposes; and, for future reference, to assess the appearance of cows on a scale of points after they had produced their first calf.

Recording the amount of milk and butterfat individual cows produced – the very thing which had by then made the Jersey

famous – was introduced gradually, and then at first only for
animals which were entered in the shows organised both by the
society itself and the agricultural societies which were beginning
to spring up in the twelve parishes. Not that proof of an ability
to produce rich milk or even of breeding consistently seems to have
mattered. By the time the Royal Jersey Agricultural and Horticultural Society was formed, the Jersey farmer had discovered
that he was on to a winner with his special breed of cattle. He could
not go wrong. It might be said that farmers from the United
Kingdom in particular but also from more distant places were
almost knocking on farmhouse doors looking for heifers or young
bulls for sale.

*   *   *

Fortune smiled twice over when the Island authorities
stopped the imports of live cattle just at a moment in history when
farmers in most advanced nations were beginning to take an
interest in improving regional types by careful breeding pro-
grammes. For it was at about this time, too, that several young
countries were beginning to open up. The most obvious and
immediately exploitable resource of some of them was vast areas
of virgin pasture. What they needed more than anything else were
stock which could transform that grass into products to be exported
for cash. They turned to sheep, beef animals – and the dairy cow.
So far as the last was concerned, fresh milk was useless because
it could not keep. But butter, preserved with salt, could be exported
to the rapidly developing urban markets almost anywhere in the
world thanks to the use of the new steam-driven ships and, in
course of time, refrigeration.

Although the milk from the Jersey cows was never regarded
as being good for making hard cheeses, before long she had come
to be recognised worldwide as the butter-producing dairy animal
par excellence. She had the extra advantages of early maturity,
of freedom from most diseases due partly to the Island breed's
isolation, a long life, an ability to cope with different kinds of
climate, and, as an added advantage for those who wanted blood-
stock bred in Jersey, proof of pedigree. Moreover, she had the

advantage those females enjoy who have style and that kind of glamorous appearance which makes them outstandingly attractive.

She went to New Zealand and Australia, to North America and India and to Africa. By 1903, when 613 head were sent to Denmark – where butter was becoming big business – there were few countries in which the Jersey could not be found.

Perhaps of all the stories the history of this tiny island has to tell, that of the Jersey cow must be among the most astonishing. As a result of the slow, unconnected unfolding of events which began with the development from ancient times of a particular kind of animal and, one must suppose, reached its peak with the expansion of vast new markets for what it was best able to produce, the Jersey smallholder made the kind of fortunes of which his forefathers could never have dreamed. But it was not fortune's smile alone that brought success. The Island farmer proved to be an outstanding breeder of fine cattle. It is not for nothing that those who even now make a speciality of the skills of selection and breeding are referred to uniquely as 'breeders'.

Even before the States imposed its first ban on imports, the name of the Channel Islands breeds had started to spread. From about 1750 onward efforts were being made as far away as the south-west of Scotland to improve the Ayrshire cattle, and it is on record that Channel Islands stock was used to do so. Probably the Scottish farmers did not know them as Jerseys or Guernseys. For a long time both were lumped together as Alderneys simply because Alderney was the last port of call for sailing ships travelling from the islands to England. The name stuck fast for years. Even in the 1920s it was used by A.A. Milne in his delightful poem for children (and grown-ups), 'The King's Breakfast'. In it the King asks, a little grumpily:

> Could we have some butter
> for the Royal slice of bread?'
> The Queen asked the Dairymaid.
> The Dairymaid said 'Certainly
> I'll go and tell the cow now,
> Before she goes to bed.'

The Dairymaid she curtsied
And went and told the Alderney
'Don't forget the butter
for the Royal slice of bread.

In the last decades of the 1700s, and perhaps even before, the Jersey was beginning to grace the farms of some of the wealthier land owners in the south of England. No doubt many of them were looking for an animal which would add distinction to their estates. Selective breeding by Island farmers enabled them to satisfy the preference of these estate owners for a cow with a deer-like appearance which included that golden-fawn colour which is still a mark of the Jersey breed. In practical terms, she was also favoured as a 'house cow', her milk being richer in flavour than that of any of the regional breeds bar, perhaps, the elephantine South Devon which was almost twice the size of the Jersey and so without any claim to comely charm.

Stevens's *Book of the Farm*, (published in 1909) mentions a 1794 report by Kent farmer John Boys. Stevens, quoting Boys, observes: 'Tests were held between a home-bred animal (probably a Suffolk) and an Alderney (sic) in which the latter produced twice the quantity of butter per gallon of milk yield.' If nothing else, that suggests that the Channel Islands breeds could by then have been seen in the south-east of England for some years at least.

Stevens goes on to suggest that 1811 marked the opening of the English commercial trade. 'In that year Mr Michael Fowler visited Jersey and commenced exporting,' he wrote. 'His practice was to take the animals to various fairs for the purpose of sale and in that way was greatly the means of popularising the breed.' Indeed, it was the business acumen of dealers like Fowler as much as the interest of large estate owners that led the Jersey breed to spread throughout much of southern England; that, and word of mouth which has always been one of the most effective forms of advertising.

In those days regular, quite often weekly, markets held in towns and villages were the centres of rural business in the United Kingdom. There, corn and livestock – and almost everything else – were bought and sold. Each market was connected with the other, and with the bigger cities, not just by atrocious highways but also a network of droving roads, now almost all gone. Great, green rivers which offered both pasture and enclosures where they could be herded at night, they were usually the means by which livestock of all kinds – cattle, sheep and even geese and wayward pigs – were driven to the markets sometimes over great distances. Almost certainly it was along these ancient droving roads that the first consignments of Jersey cattle were taken from one market to the next until the last had been sold.

The dealers must have taken some of them a considerable distance in search of a profitable sale. There have been suggestions that, like draught oxen which were then quite frequently still being used for road work, some animals were even shod with light iron plates to save their hooves from damage on long treks. Perhaps it is not surprising that the Jersey cow never did become popular in the north of England. Few got there – simply because there was more pain to be found in trudging that far than there was profit.

Records from other sources suggest that Stevens was badly out when he claimed that Fowler, although perhaps the first English dealer to buy speculatively, 'opened the English trade' in 1811. Henry Inglis, writing twenty-four years later about the Island, remarked: 'In 1810 and the three following years 3,050 head were exported.' There is no reason to doubt Inglis, and that level of business must be proof that by the time Fowler began operations the Jersey-bred animal was already in great demand in England. Inglis went on to note that in the three years ending in 1832, 5,756 head were exported. He added that 'prices have dropped in the past fifteen years and are now from £8 to £10, but some sell for £15.'

To give an idea of the level of profits that were already being made from this new trade at that level of prices, he was writing at a time when the daily wage of a master carpenter was 3s.6d, a day labourer 1s.6d to 2s, and a woman employed to weed crops a mere 6d. Thus for a master carpenter to buy a cow for £10 would have meant parting with ten weeks' full wages – and a weeder of crops over a year's work!

It is close to impossible these days to grasp the commercial significance of the Island's cattle export business, or its scale, during the whole of the 1800s. The great majority of the stock went to enthusiastic buyers in the United Kingdom. But as early as 1817 the first animal was exported to distant America. By the 1850s regular consignments were being sent (now often by steamships) to the United States, which in terms of both demand and price was to prove to be one of the most lucrative and dependable markets. In 1854 the first recorded consignment went even further – to Australia. Eight years later New Zealand took some. That year – 1860 – 1,138 head were sent to England alone at an average price of £16. In 1880 a number were shipped to South Africa; and in that same year Ansted reported that prices of up to £400 per head were being paid. Two years later a young cow, 'Khedive's Princess', was bought by an American for the record price of £1,000. The following year 250 head were exported to Sweden. In 1903, 613 head were sent to Denmark in three shipments. So great was the continuing demand from all sources that it proved impossible to meet a request by the Danes for a fourth consignment. And alongside these larger consignments, of course, there were individual contracts with enthusiastic breeders in the United Kingdom and elsewhere.

*   *   *

But to go back a little. By the 1820s Jersey had become the British equivalent of Boom Town USA. There was a merchant fleet of imposing size sailing the world. There was smuggling and privateering. The Newfoundland cod fisheries were thriving. The waters around the east of the Island were about to become the scene of a mad scramble for oysters. Everywhere, it seems now, there was profit waiting for those willing to grab it from the sea.

The Island's great maritime days, however, were shortly to come to an end, whittled away by changing circumstances. Jersey's fleet of wooden ships and the coastal shipyards where many of them were built eventually found themselves unable to compete with iron and steam. Napoleon's final defeat in 1815 brought peace between Britain and France and an end to privateering in local waters. In 1810 an English Customs house was established in Jersey which had some effect on the contraband trade. Greed destroyed the oyster beds for ever.

In the countryside, however, there were fortunes yet to be made. They no longer came only from the great quantities of cider that were still being produced but also from the Island breed of cow and, later, the early potato; and later still from the field-grown tomato. Right through the 1800s and into the first half of the next century, farming in Jersey enjoyed the greatest period of prosperity it had ever known; and may perhaps never know again. As for the cattle trade, so great was the demand by overseas buyers for well-bred animals that time and again fears were expressed that the quality of the Island's foundation breeding stock was bound to suffer through the loss of the best. That, however, did nothing to put a brake on things.

In 1781, James Playfair, writing generally about the Island smallholder, remarked in a guesswork kind of way: 'He keeps a horse and two cows.' That proportion was to alter dramatically. Records show that in 1866 – the year the Jersey Herd Book was founded – there were 3,227 horses and 12,037 head of cattle (including bulls and heifers). The latter figure suggests that the average size of herd on the average smallholding had then risen to about six.

It was in the late 1800s that the failing cider industry began to be replaced by a quite new product – the early potato. However, the demand for cattle stayed at a high level. They and potatoes, together with a plentiful supply of cheap labour – and hard work – enabled generations of Jersey farmers to continue to maintain an astonishing level of prosperity despite the small size of their holdings, and even during the slump years of United Kingdom agriculture in the last decades of the century.

Crowned heads came and went. Victoria died. Edward VII reigned briefly. George V, his successor, held the throne until he, too, died. When George VI was crowned in 1936 following the abdication of his brother, the Island's farming stock must have enjoyed the placid belief that despite some problems they lived in settled times. Still farming in much the same style as their smallholder forebears had done, they had a reasonable income – perhaps in some years a very considerable profit – from potatoes, the outdoor tomatoes grown from the early 1900s on the lighter soils and, in particular, from the cattle they sold and the milk their small herds produced.

After the Occupation it seemed, in the euphoria and innocence of peace, that agriculture would return to the precise point where it had been before the outbreak of the war. It was not to be, either for farming in Jersey in general or for the breeder. True, in 1948, 2,041 head of cattle – the highest number ever exported in one year – left for new homes. The Island herd returned to its pre-war level of about ten thousand head. But times were changing faster than anybody in Jersey could have forecast. Dairy farmers overseas, once so enthusiastic but now with their own pool of animals to breed from, became increasingly reluctant to buy expensive beasts from the breed's foundation stock, and to transport them, often at great cost by air, over long distances. Besides, there was this new thing, artificial insemination, which made it possible to improve herds without any need to buy a live animal outright. Then there came to be an over-production of butter by the world's producers which led to falling prices on international markets. And finally, quite suddenly, much publicity was given to claims that the kind of fats contained in milk and butter were harmful to the human system. The warnings were noted by increasingly health-conscious nations, who turned instead to using low-fat milk and vegetable oils rather than animal fats. Inevitably, all these factors had their effect on local sales.

The Jersey cow was no longer a darling of the world pursued by suitors; and her products came under the scrutiny of suspicion. With each small flicker of interest from foreign buyers – when in 1958, for example, a consignment of cattle was sent to what was then Yugoslavia, or when seventy-four head were sent to Turkey in 1967 – there may have come renewed hope that overseas sales might revive. They never did. Slowly the export trade in live animals began to tail off. The Island's cattlemen, their numbers decreasing as each year passed, were obliged to look more and more towards the sale of fresh milk within the community as the main – although modest – source of income from their herds. It was no longer possible to hope to make a profit from just a few cosseted cows, either in terms of live sales or of the milk they produced.

By 1976 the Island herd had dropped to just over seven

thousand head. By 1991 the total had fallen to 6,517, a half of what it had been in 1866. Where formerly almost every farmer had owned a few cows, by 1991 there remained only seventy-nine registered milk producers in Jersey, with numbers falling annually; not breeders, mark you, as they once were, just milk producers whose incomes had to be protected by subsidies and a ban on the importation of fresh milk.

For over a hundred and fifty years the Jersey cow brought prosperity to many and a gentle kind of fame to the Island. Hers is a remarkable achievement unequalled by any breed of dairy animal in any part of the world. Maybe that is a fitting tribute to all those generations of Island smallholders whose skill as breeders had helped to make it possible. Or perhaps an epitaph. For unless good fortune arrives in some other guise, the export trade in live cattle, while it still continues, must be considered moribund.

But it was good while it lasted.

10.

Plant them in your worst ground

EVERYBODY KNOWS that Sir Walter Raleigh, noted in a previous chapter as Jersey's most famous Governor, although far from the most effective, is widely believed to have introduced the potato to Europe. He probably did so following his expedition to South America in 1595. In terms of bringing back booty, his second expedition to that part of the American continent was less successful and proved to be disastrous for Raleigh. On his return he was accused by James I of treason, was imprisoned (for the second time) and was finally executed in 1618.

At first the potato was regarded merely as an interesting novelty. Grown exclusively in the gardens of the wealthy, not surprisingly it was thought of as nothing more than a strange plant whose tubers might be eaten by the venturesome. It did not merit special treatment. 'Plant them in your worst ground,' advised John Evelyn, the seventeenth-century English diarist, who was himself a keen gardener. But its potential as food for the people of England, as elsewhere in Europe, was quickly recognised by some. By 1662, only forty-four years after Raleigh's death, the English Royal Agricultural Society was encouraging the commercial development of the potato as an alternative kind of produce lest 'there be a famine or a failure of the corn crop'.

Despite this recommendation, recognition that there was profit to be made from this new vegetable caught on only slowly in the countryside. So did the twin idea among the population itself of actually eating not a root but a tuber (something never done before) brought originally from a fabulous place months of sailing distant. However, by the 1730s the potato was starting to be

123

cultivated on certain farms in the United Kingdom and to appear on the markets. Almost certainly it was being grown commercially before then, although on a limited scale.

The potato must surely have arrived in Jersey at about the same period as it did in England, quite likely being grown in the gardens of certain interested seigneurs. According to Thomas Quayle, writing in 1818, when it first appeared in the Island it was regarded more as 'an object of curiosity than otherwise....and was very roughly attended to'. At that time potato blight and the virus diseases which were to cause so many problems for future generations of farmers and gardeners were quite unknown. The crop, planted in virgin soil made rich over the centuries by good husbandry and without a single enemy to worry about, thrived remarkably. Recording his memories six decades later, Jerseyman C.P.Le Cornu wrote in 1880: 'I can remember before the setting in of the potato disease having seen the haulms rise above the ground as high as the surrounding hedges.' When he went out hunting in the autumn, he added, his dogs would disappear entirely in the vegetation, which was so thick that when it had died back it was collected and used as fuel for fires.

At first it was probably relegated to odd, unused spots, for example the open verges of apple orchards. The Jersey smallholder, sticking to the things he knew and more interested in making cider, had little time for this new-fangled potato, no doubt preferring the trustworthy parsnip. Quayle remarks: 'It was a dirty and ill cared for crop...and largely used for fattening hogs and stock for market.' The tubers were 'large coarse and knotty'. By the end of the 1700s, however, with improved strains appearing and with interest in it as a food for humans increasing throughout Europe, it was clearly becoming something that might be worth growing commercially.

The first known report of exports of potatoes from Jersey, 'forty to fifty cargoes in vessels of fifty tons burthen' comes in a record dated 1807. The quantity which left the Island was in the order of a surprising six hundred tons. So great a quantity suggests that potatoes had, in fact, been grown commercially for export for some time before that. By 1811 exports had just about doubled. The Jersey smallholder, still producing great quantities of cider and now on the edge of being involved in a thriving trade in cattle, was nevertheless clearly quick to develop the potential of yet a third means of making a profit from his small patches of land.

The main market must have been the United Kingdom, including what one report referred to as 'the mining districts of England'. But thanks to the existence of the Island's great mercantile fleet (due shortly to vanish as steam took over from sail) consignments of Jersey potatoes were sent to Portugal, to Gibraltar and possibly other parts of the Mediterranean. They even went to Guernsey and, for some reason, to distant Brazil – quite probably included in a cargo of the salted cod that had originally been caught on the Grand Banks off Newfoundland.

One advantage of the potato is that it is easy to breed new varieties. From the time it came to be recognised as a significant food crop, efforts must have been made to produce strains that gave higher yields and a better quality of tuber. Perhaps because of the benefit of a mild climate the Jersey farmer preferred what had come to be called the 'early' varieties, that is those which could be dug mature during August and September. There were a number of popular kinds. Some bore the name of the breeder, such as the Stayner, some suggested shape or colour, for example the Jersey Blues. And there was even one that for an obscure reason was given the name of 'Les Dégenérées'. From export figures alone it is clear that the potato was proving profitable. In 1842, for example, over 18,000 tons of these 'early maincrop' potatoes were grown and exported.

* * *

Then disaster struck. Exactly how the potato blight fungus developed is uncertain, although it is known that it first appeared in the United States in 1843. Perhaps its spread worldwide was connected with the large areas of the crop that were now being grown which allowed the invisible spores to leapfrog rapidly from one patch to another over huge areas. Whatever the reason, it was new. It was something nobody had ever experienced before. It spread rapidly – apparently with no regard for distances. Once a grower found evidence of its presence, nothing could be done to prevent it wiping out, or nearly so, a crop that had a total lack of resistance and whose soft, sappy foliage provided ideal conditions for the disease to develop. There was no cure. It arrived silently and implacably like some awful vegetable plague.

In Ireland, where a mild, damp climate had encouraged farmers to grow great quantities of potatoes, often to the exclusion of such other foodstuffs as corn, the appearance of the blight and the subsequent failure of the crop in the early 1840s led to a human disaster on a terrible scale. Late and reluctantly, the British government was forced to provide aid. But it has been said that as a consequence of the ruin caused by the disease some twelve per cent of Ireland's population died from the effects of under-nourishment or downright starvation during what was to be called throughout Britain with descriptive exactness the Hungry Forties. Much of Europe and most of Britain was affected by this untreatable fungus disease. It appeared in Jersey in June, 1845.

For the Island's smallholders the consequences, although far from being a matter of life and death as they were for the Irish, were commercially serious. The knitted stocking trade had ended and the cider trade was dying slowly. And while the Jersey cow was selling to eager overseas buyers at high prices, farmers had begun to depend heavily on the potato crop for a considerable part of their income. Some smallholders gave up bothering and reverted to growing parsnips for fattening stock, 'but this was found to answer only as a temporary relief'. Others turned to a variety of potato called 'the pink eye' which cropped heavily but was of very inferior quality. Maybe it, too, was used primarily for feeding livestock rather than for export to English markets.

The years passed by. The virulence of the blight seems to have diminished a little and copper compounds, which it had been discovered gave some protection, were starting to be used on what crops were grown. Despite the damage caused by the fungus, which could not be treated once it had taken a hold, and other soil-borne diseases which caused the tubers to rot, potatoes were now an essential foodstuff in many parts of Europe and were arriving on the English markets from various sources in annually greater quantities. But it is easy to suppose that coming after so promising a start, the initial setback caused by the arrival of blight, together perhaps with lower profits due to greater production in the United Kingdom, left the Jersey smallholder thinking that there was little future for the kind of early maincrop potato he had been growing.

It took the foresight and entrepreneurial energy of prosperous St Ouen farmer John Le Caudey to lift potato growers out of whatever despondency they may have fallen into, and to set Island agriculture on a new and very profitable course. In 1858, thirteen years after the blight first arrived in Jersey and with the future seeming to be so uncertain, he came to the conclusion that the south-facing slopes of a British island with a mild climate should be ideally suited to growing crops of really early potatoes which could be got on to the English markets well before others grown anywhere else in Britain. Early enough too, perhaps, to reduce the risk of infection by blight. With fortune smiling yet again, Le Caudey's brainwave came at just the right moment. Steamships which could carry cargoes of such tender, perishable produce swiftly and certainly had by now come into use on the Jersey-United Kingdom route, while the rapidly expanding network of railways could take the goods on with equal speed to many inland markets. At the same time, increasing prosperity in Britain was making it possible for people with quite modest incomes to buy what had once been luxury products raised under glass.

A number of Island farmers became interested in Le Caudey's idea. Seemingly indefatigable and evidently with the financial means to do so, he himself went to England, Scotland and France in search of the earliest and most suitable varieties of potato and to discuss shipping and marketing arrangements with merchants and others. Things moved ahead swiftly, for on April 16 the following year the first small consignment of the first truly early Jersey potatoes was sent off on the steamship Metropolis. So great did the demand prove to be that two additional vessels were called into service.

*   *   *

The first full cargoes were shipped in June, one to Swansea on the 13th and the other to London on the 17th. The era of the

Jersey early potato trade had arrived. By 1864 some 4,000 tons of potatoes were being harvested, excluding the quantity kept back for seed. The next year production was up to 7,900 tons. The total value of the exported crop that season was £55,000. That may not sound an extraordinary sum. On the other hand, only a short time previously the future for the trade had looked dismal. Besides, those were the days when a bottle of brandy cost 1s 6d and six bottles of sherry could be bought for 12s 6d. By 1869, over 6,100 vergées of potatoes were being grown. Six years later the area had risen to more than 9,000 vergées. Shipments in 1874 amounted to 20,000 tons; the following year – only sixteen years after the first small consignments had left the Island – to 28,000 tons.

Presumably the greater part of the exports were truly 'earlies', although there are no records to show whether by then Island growers had moved entirely away from exporting the early main-crop varieties. What is certain is that well before then Jersey had become an island devoted not only to the local breed of cow but also to the early potato, for which demand on the markets was reflected in the high prices that could be obtained. No longer grown exclusively in the favoured sun-warmed côtils, they could now be seen everywhere thriving in the fertile soil of the protected, high-banked fields.

Le Caudey brought another special benefit to the Jersey smallholder. He introduced the use of 'guano'. The material was actually the droppings of the multitudes of sea-fishing birds breeding off rocks along the western coast of South America. The material had built up in vast quantities over the ages and, its value in improving crops having been established, the deposits were first mined in 1804. It was imported into the UK as a fertiliser from 1820. Le Caudey impressed on his colleagues that the product, immensely rich in plant foods such as phosphates, should be used liberally on land to be planted to potatoes.

The results were well illustrated in a trial carried out by a grower in 1867 when guano was sown on one plot at 300 lb. a vergée but none on another. The former gave a crop of potatoes fifty per cent greater than did the latter. The use of guano caught on very quickly, for by 1874 some one thousand tons were being imported into Jersey. The Peruvian deposits were finally worked out a short time later. By then, however, the kind of 'artificial' fertilisers used these days were coming on to the markets, although even now some farmers still refer to this material by the old name of 'guano'.

It was not just the use of fertilisers which ensured bountiful, and profitable, crops. The land had been made rich and fertile over the generations by hard labour and good farming practices to the point at which, in 1835 (admittedly a decade before the potato blight first appeared but long before the use of guano), Henry Inglis was able to report from his own investigations that the yield of what were then maincrop potatoes in Jersey was 5.75 tons per vergée compared with about four tons in the Isle of Wight. Sixty years later Ansted, referring to the early potato, estimated the yield, aided by the use of guano, at just over six tons a vergée.

The extraordinary amount of care and work that was put into preparing the land for the crop during the latter part of the 1800s was remarked upon by a M. Henri Johanet, who held the prestigious title of *Adminstrateur de la Société des Agriculteurs de France*. Writing in 1883, he told society members how the land was first shallow-ploughed (these days called breezing, an anglicisation of the Jersey Norman-French word *brassie*) to turn in any weeds and the manure or *vraic* which had been spread on the soil. Later it was ploughed – and then ploughed again, this time so deep (and sometimes requiring a team of eight horses to do so) that it actually turned up the subsoil. The aim, one must suppose, was to place the rich surface soil far down in order to encourage the growth of the plant's roots.

Such pains to achieve perfection suggest not just that the early potato was hugely profitable but also that the smallholder's prosperity was still dependent on getting all he could from his land without thought for the labour involved. Of course, the steeper south-facing *côtils* where the crop was originally grown were still being dug by hand with a spade – something which continued until well into the 1950s. By then, though, profits and labour costs began to make the use of some of this land quite uneconomic so that while many are still intensively cultivated – more usually now with a plough hauled by a cable on a winch – others have been allowed to revert to nature.

'The steep, south-facing côtils where the crop was originally grown.'

It was shortly before M. Johanet's visit that the story of the Island's early potato industry took another turn. Back in 1870 the benefits Le Caudey had brought to potato growers were given public recognition. By all accounts a kind and gentle man, he was invited to attend a formal ceremony where he was presented with a purse of 150 golden guineas – an amount which indicates a firm return to farming prosperity – together with a gold watch and chain and a testimonial signed by a great number of grateful Islanders.

While for some reason his name is now rarely mentioned in connection with what is still Jersey's most important field-grown crop, that of Hugh de la Haye appears frequently.

*   *   *

Exactly ten years after Le Caudey was honoured, de la Haye, a bachelor who lived at Bushy Farm, Mont Cochon, walked into a potato merchant's store which Le Caudey had opened on The Esplanade in St Helier. There, displayed on the office counter for the sake of passing interest, were two huge potatoes grown by a local farmer whose name has never been recorded. De la Haye asked to have them. It is said that shortly afterwards, during the meal always given by farmers to those who had helped with their corn harvest, he showed the tubers to his friends. They suggested that he should plant them. One had an astonishing sixteen 'eyes', or embryo shoots. Following the quite common practice of the times, de la Haye cut the potatoes so that each piece contained one of these growing shoots. Later, he planted them in a field he cultivated in Bellozanne Valley.

Right from the outset a number of different varieties of early potato had been bred from seed and grown on, among them a kidney-shaped type called The Fluke, itself a variation of the widely-grown (but dauntingly named) Jersey Kidney. Evidently those nurtured by de la Haye were of this kind. By 1884 he had harvested enough to exhibit a basketful of them in the office window of the bi-weekly newspaper *La Nouvelle Chronique*.

At that time Victoria, *regina et imperatrix*, was adored by a nation to the extent that it bestowed her name on anything it reasonably could – from a London railway station to a plum, from a horse-drawn carriage to a newly-constructed Jersey road. Perhaps fortunately the newspaper's proprietor, Charles Le Feuvre (the author's grandfather), instead of calling de la Haye's potatoes 'Victorias', gave them the name of the Royal Jersey Fluke. And the Royal it still remains.

Exactly why the potatoes raised by de la Haye from the originals he was given should have proved to be so superior to all the others that were being grown then is uncertain. Possibly it was the taste, or the earliness, or – with its shallow eyes and clean, golden skin – the appearance. Indeed, it remains a mystery why they should have differed from some others since there is no evidence to suggest that they had been raised from seed as a quite new kind. Almost certainly one factor which made the Royal Jersey Fluke commercially interesting was its ability to resist the virus diseases that cause many other varieties to degenerate and so eventually render them useless. The Royal's resistance to viral infections, together with careful selection by careful growers over the years, makes it possible even now for each farmer to hold back perhaps a fifth or a quarter of one year's crop to provide the material for the next. It is a kind of benevolent perpetual motion denied to many other potato growers in Europe. But although to grow enough tubers for the next year's planting is useful, there is a yet greater hidden advantage. While early and maincrop varieties in scores or hundreds have appeared on local markets and elsewhere – and vanished as a result of slow deterioration through virus diseases – the Royal has so far been grown steadily and exclusively in the Island for over one hundred and ten consecutive years. That is a remarkable record for any vegetable – perhaps any plant. The unvarying consistency of type from year to year for such a long period is surely one reason why the Jersey Royal still remains a favourite on United Kingdom markets.

Like Le Caudey, Hugh de la Haye was something of a hero in his time. He was presented with an illuminated address and a purse of golden sovereigns by admiring farmers and others. Both men, intentionally or otherwise, played a great part in ensuring the prosperity of Island agriculture perhaps more so than even the most able of the cattle breeders.

*   *   *

But to go back a little; by the time de la Haye exhibited his produce in the newspaper's window, farming in the Island had undergone a transformation. The cider export trade was just about dead and orchards were being grubbed up to make way for the potato or for pasture for the profitable Jersey cow. Where at one time the smallholder had been reasonably content to put some emphasis on individual self-sufficiency from his land rather than cash profits, he had by now moved firmly into the world of commerce. Where, before, he had grown enough corn to meet little more than his own needs, or enough parsnips to feed his livestock and his family, or enough hay to feed his horse and cattle, he was now concentrating his efforts on producing goods for sale.

The growth of the potato trade, coming as it did at about the same time as the growth in the cattle export trade, marked a radical change in rural attitudes. The smallholder could no longer be described as a peasant who saw his land primarily as a means of maintaining his independence and sustaining himself and his family through what he grew. He had become a farmer in the modern sense; perhaps on a small scale, but a farmer nevertheless.

The extent to which the farming community had become dependent on outside sources in a desire to grow for export produce that brought in a greater profit might be seen in the fact that in 1886 alone 1,100 tons of hay, 100 tons of straw and 3,000 tons of 'guano' were imported from England. Such a turn of events would have been unthinkable at the start of the century.

In 1891 the Island's farmers, now heavily dependent on Breton labour, exported 66,840 tons of potatoes, bringing a gross income of £487,642. (By comparison, one might recall, the 1868 figures had been 7,890 tons and £55,000 respectively.) But not all seasons were as remarkable as that of '91. Some were exceptional but some were a disaster. Sometimes the weather was poor, sometimes a late frost damaged huge areas of the crop, sometimes the markets were unsteady. However, the Jersey Royal and the Jersey cow made a marvellous partnership. The potato could be dug early enough to enable roots to be grown as a second crop to feed the cattle, while the livestock improved the fertility of the soil in which potatoes were to be grown. Both brought their share of profit even to farmers who had only a little land. They, together with tomatoes, were to continue to do so, ensuring a quite remarkable degree of prosperity for the farming community and forming what one might reasonably call the *raison d'être* of Island agriculture from the early 1800s right through the first half of the 1900s.

The speed at which both cattle and potatoes came to dominate Island agriculture from the late 1800s to the start of the Second World War is nothing short of astonishing. Unfortunately, it is a period often taken as the benchmark by which later standards of Jersey's agricultural prosperity continue to be measured by some. It is difficult to imagine what might have happened to the Island without their presence. By comparison with almost any other part of Britain, the wealth they brought to the smallholder for a century and a half was quite out of proportion to the area of the land he worked. Because, unlike the more tender tomato, it could be grown on any soil with more or less success (depending on the seasons), the Jersey Royal continued to be the most important field-grown crop for export. In 1930, at the start of the years of what came to be called the Great Depression following the Wall Street market collapse, the area planted to earlies was 17,337 vergées; in 1939, 22,099 vergées. That was an area probably never to be exceeded again.

The end of the German Occupation brought hope to the potato grower, and the farming community in general, that things would return to the way they had been before. And so they did – for a while. But in the years that followed, labour, particularly from the traditional source of Brittany, became scarcer as work became more easily available in the region. There was also increasing competition on the United Kingdom early potato markets from growers in other countries as far apart as Egypt and the Canary Islands. Though lacking the quality of the Jersey Royal, these imports were early, and they were cheap. The low price of this foreign produce, and increasing wages demanded in Jersey by fewer available workers, were two of the factors which began slowly to make it clear that although it was the best way of harvesting such a tender crop, digging potatoes by hand with a fork and a gang of three people was coming to be just too expensive. It was time for machinery to begin to take over.

There were many other problems that affected Island agriculture after the Second World War, some common to all farmers and not just the potato grower. They are outlined in broad detail in a later chapter. It is enough to remark here that so far as the smallholder was concerned, he was slowly forced to realise that he could no longer depend on an income the greater part of which came from perhaps fifteen or twenty vergées of early potatoes (and in many cases far fewer). Some tried other crops – anemones, parsley, more narcissi, cauliflowers, calabrese, courgettes – in the hope that diversity would be an answer. For a while trials were held of other varieties of early potato, but none was successful.

Right from the start, the cultivation of early potatoes has been recognised as being both a risky and expensive business. There is always the chance of late spring frosts, of disease, of too much rain or too little, of gluts on United Kingdom markets causing prices to plummet almost overnight. Despite all the problems, however, no other market garden crop has yet been found which could replace the Jersey Royal entirely. It is the foundation on which Island agriculture still rests. So the Royal continues to reign, although now frequently given shelter in its youthful days under clear plastic to encourage even earlier maturity.

During the five years 1987 to 1991 inclusive, an average total of some 14,600 vergées were grown each year. Exports during that period amounted to an annual average of 33,100 tons, bringing a gross average return of over £17.6m. Figures like that indicate that not all is doom and gloom, particularly in the case of a vegetable whose field life is little more than a brief twelve weeks or so and which can therefore be followed by a second cash crop providing one can be found that is commercially profitable.

Over a run of seasons, the potato grower can still gain an income; but not the level of profits that the Jersey Royal once provided in such abundance. Whether it can continue to provide reasonable dividends in relation to the capital and the labour involved in growing it is a matter for conjecture, if not doubt.

135

11.

Summer sun
shines on Jersey Tom

PUBLICITY AGENTS would say that as a product of the Jersey soil the outdoor tomato has never enjoyed a very positive image. Cider-making, the Jersey breed of cow and the Jersey Royal potato have all become an admired part of local history. They are immediately recognisable symbols of the Island's countryside both among the local population and with tourists. They have achieved a status, an image, and have edged their way into local traditions. On the other hand Jersey Tom, as its promoters have named it without too much success, has never been granted any similar level of honour either within the Island or elsewhere.

General reference books make only passing mention of tomatoes. Records are sparse even in the more serious publications. Yet for a while it may have seemed to some that the field-grown tomato could become the most important, and certainly potentially the most profitable, of Jersey's export crops. For a few, they did actually bring considerable wealth.

Tomatoes, as grown out of doors, are relative newcomers on the Island's farming scene. First cultivated *en plein air* for export in the last part of the 1800s or at the turn of the century, they had been raised commercially under glass for a number of years before that. It took several alert Island farmers to realise that Jersey's mild climate meant that they might equally well be grown in the open, and far more cheaply since there was no need for the expensive glasshouse protection it had always been thought necessary to provide.

Among those credited with introducing them as a field crop was Mr Paul Lamy, of St Saviour, who learnt about their culture while working on a farm in the American state of Iowa and brought the skills back with him. Another was Mr J.P. Le Masurier, of St Clement. Like others, he tried out several of many varieties of the fruit, including the Jambart Beauty, the Flying Dutch, the Frogmore and the Sunrise. This last was to become the outstanding favourite among growers, merchants and the buying public, and was to remain so until some time after the end of the last war. In terms of quality as a dessert fruit it is still considered by a few to be the best variety of all.

As with the early potato, Jersey quickly proved to be well suited for the cultivation of tomatoes. Except in bad years, the climate favoured a plant which needs heat, sunshine and not too much rain; and the Island lay close enough to the United Kingdom to enable perishable fruit like a tomato to reach the markets in perfect condition. Moreover, the smallholder was by now skilled in caring for market garden crops which needed personal attention if they were to thrive, and local merchants in selling them on to English wholesalers at the best prices.

There were two other special advantages for the Island's smallholders. The introduction of tomatoes into the range of crops grown in Jersey proved as attractive in one way to the Breton seasonal workers – found on most farms until the 1950s and upon whom the growers entirely depended – as it did to their employers in another. At one time the Bretons came on a contract of perhaps no more than six weeks merely to dig the early potato crop, to help with the hay harvest and hoe the root crops. They were also available to deal with the *branchage*, the compulsory bi-annual trimming of roadside banks and hedgerows which in Jersey is the responsibility of individual landowners and tenants.

Now they had a chance to make what to them was a great deal of money by working *à tache* (piecework) in both the potato and tomato fields right through until the last of the fruit had been harvested in the late autumn. Not surprisingly, therefore, if they had a choice it would be to work for a grower who had tomatoes rather than for somebody who had none. Quite apart from the potential for profit from the crop, it was a situation which gave indirect encouragement to the industry to expand by applying pressure on some farmers to plant the crop on land which, as it

'Jersey's mild climate meant that tomatoes could be grown successfully in the open fields.'

happened, in the end quite often proved not to be suitable. The other advantage even now is that the tomato has a kind of flexibility. It can be grown either as a main crop or as a second crop planted out immediately after those early potatoes which it has been possible to lift from the field in May. Thus, providing the situation is suitable, there is the opportunity of a twofold cash income from the same patch of land.

As with the Jersey Royal, outdoor-grown tomatoes began to arrive on the English markets just at a time when an increasing, and increasingly prosperous, middle class could indulge itself in the luxuries of fresh produce at reasonable prices. And, it might be added, it provided a new export product for local smallholders at the moment in Island history when the great era of cider-making had come to an end.

*   *   *

What statistics there are available show that from a standing start, as it were, the tomato proved to be an immediate winner. Between 1903 and 1909 the average of exports from the Island was over 2,100 tons a year. Unfortunately, these figures do not differentiate between produce grown under glass and that grown in the fields. But one can at least get some idea of the speed with which the industry developed by looking at the extraordinary increase in the quantities exported from then on. In the six years between 1910 and 1916 the average of annual exports rose to very nearly 7,400 tons. From the mid-1920s to 1930, the figure was 17,300 tons.

That is an astonishing quantity of fruit, particularly in view of the fact that by 1930 tomatoes had been cultivated commercially as a field crop for no more than thirty-five years. Besides, the smallholder was at the same time also in the other profitable businesses of exporting great quantities of early potatoes and raising cattle for which at the time there was still an almost insatiable demand worldwide.

It is only from 1930 onward, when the Island's Department of Agriculture began to publish annual sets of statistics, that one can begin to visualise the significance of the industry in so small a place as Jersey. That year there were just about 1,150 vergées of field-grown tomatoes planted as first crop and just under 2,000 vergées grown as second crop. There was a further 71 vergées grown under glass.

By then annual exports had risen to over twenty thousand tons. The explosion of interest was to continue right up to the start of the Second World War. In 1939 a total of 6,678 vergées of tomatoes was grown – more than double the area of that recorded nine years before – with exports totalling 31,000 tons. The gross value was £400,000.

Clearly, the Jersey tomato had become a favourite on the English markets. For one thing, there was no competition from low-cost, field-grown crops in the United Kingdom. For another, fruit grown out of doors always has a markedly better flavour than when grown in a glasshouse. And for yet another, the favoured varieties such as the Sunrise, the Potato Leaf and the Devon, with their thin skins and lusciously juicy centres, quickly came to be recognised as fruit that was just as excellent when eaten alone or in salads as with the morning's fried eggs and bacon. So, too, had the crop become a favourite among Island growers. It flourished best on the lighter, sandier soils, and the summer sun shone on vistas of tomato fields in the most favourable areas of the eastern parishes of Grouville and St Clement in particular, and in the west in the parish of St Ouen at L'Etacq and Val de la Mare and in the parish of St Brelade. But tomatoes were also to be found growing in all the other Island parishes, especially where there were warm, south-facing slopes.

A field of tomatoes is marginally less attractive to the eye of the passer-by than rows of vines in a vineyard, and almost certainly needs a great deal more labour. Depending on the method favoured by the grower, each plant requires either a bamboo stake support or to be trained up strings suspended from overhead wires running the length of each row. Whichever system is favoured, the plants need almost constant attention. Apart from hoeing and regular spraying to protect against blight, the main shoots of every plant must be tied under each flower truss to hold the stem firm to its support; side shoots must be pulled off; the growing tip must be removed, usually when the third truss appears, to encourage a limited crop of the best quality; and the lower leaves must be taken off as they die back in order to allow the sun to reach the bottom trusses of the plant. And, of course, during the harvesting period the crop must be gone through time after time so that the individual fruits can be picked as they ripen. Then there is the sorting, the grading, the packing in twelve pound trays, the transporting to the cargo ships berthed in St Helier harbour. But despite the immense amount of labour involved, the Jersey tomato was providing healthy profits for many and fortunes for some – to the extent that in the years immediately after the break in normal life caused by the German Occupation, growers threw themselves back into the business with even greater enthusiasm than before.

In 1946, just under 29,000 tons were exported at a value of £1.7m. The next year exports shot up to 44,500 tons, valued at £2.7m. In 1948, when the early potato crop brought in a gross return of just under £1.2m, the value of the 35,000 tons of tomatoes exported was £3m. Translated into current values, that £3m can hardly be far short of – and is possibly more than – a quite remarkable £100m gross return.

*   *   *

At this point it must have seemed to some people that despite ever-uncertain markets and Britain's fickle climate, even at its southernmost edge, the future of Island horticulture lay more with the tomato than the Jersey Royal. But a warning came in 1951 from a Frenchman, Dr Pierre Dalido, who wrote in, *Ile Agricole Anglo-Normande* (in translation): 'It seems there is an exaggerated enthusiasm for tomatoes, and many farmers are planting them in areas which do not suit them...It is likely that fewer tomatoes will be grown in the years ahead and that little by little the potato will return to the position it formerly held.' So it quickly proved to be. By 1958 the area of the outdoor crop had dropped to 4,700 vergées, and by 1969 to 2,627 vergées. In that year field-grown tomatoes accounted for only £1.2m of the £10.2m gross income from crops exported from Jersey, of which £1m came from fruit raised under glass.

There were several reasons for the decline. During the boom years some tomato crops had been grown in such unsuitable areas that, as wholesalers became more choosy, the poor quality of the fruit gathered from them, and consequently the low prices they achieved, meant that there was little or no profit to be made. Labour, too, was becoming scarcer and more expensive. At the same time, competition from foreign produce on the United Kingdom markets was increasing every year. And, of course this was the era which saw the growth of supermarkets whose prime demand, so it has been said, was for produce to display that was colourful and regular in shape. Field-grown produce, although more tasty, could not always measure up to the supermarket buyers' rigorous requirements.

But the day of the Jersey outdoor tomato is far from over. In 1991, more than 290 vergées were grown as first crop and 90 vergées as second crop. Their harvest, together with that from the hundred-odd vergées raised under glass, brought in £5.8m. However, the boom years, when large areas of the countryside were transformed into tiny forests of four-foot bamboo canes, when hundreds of Breton workers tended the crops and when scores of lively Welsh girls arrived each summer to sort and pack the fruit for export – and money was to be made almost too easily from what had once been called the 'love apple' – have long gone. And no doubt there will be those who, with tastebuds attuned to former times or who can grow their own, will say that the foreign-grown, ready-packaged, cling-film product to be seen now on many supermarket shelves at any time of the year is but a travesty of what a real tomato should be.

12.
The changes that came silently and unannounced

FARMING in the United Kingdom changed radically during the Second World War. In its quite different way the transformation was as profound as anything that had occurred in Britain during the Industrial Revolution, and occurred far more swiftly. A sudden dependence on home-grown food lifted British agriculture out of the depression it had suffered during the inter-war years and gave it a rejuvenating injection of vitality. There were new ideas, new ways of doing things with far fewer people, a better understanding and the provision of preferential treatment from a government aware that in war food is as vital as munitions. Science and engineering made possible the introduction of immensely important innovations such as combine harvesters, selective weed-killers, artificial insemination and hydraulic lifts fitted on light, mobile tractors to which new kinds of implements could be attached directly instead of being dragged cumbersomely behind.

In Jersey, on the other hand, the German Occupation turned the people into prisoners isolated from events in the outside world. They had no opportunity to learn about the changes going on elsewhere, or any means of benefiting from them if they did. Controls and shortages of every kind forced the farming community to continue as it had done, if not actually to revert to an almost medieval way of doing things.

It was natural for them to suppose, then, that with peace, farming in the Island would continue where it had left off at the outbreak of the war. For a brief while there was no reason to suspect it might be otherwise. Aided by generously high producer prices fixed by the British government, early potatoes were in great

143

demand among an English population so long denied such luxuries. There was an astonishing boom in the production of outdoor
tomatoes. In 1948 alone over two thousand head of cattle, the
greatest number ever sold overseas in one year, left the Island.
The smallholder was doing nicely once more and could disregard
what was happening elsewhere. Traditional methods, it appeared,
were as firmly back in place as the arrival each May of the Breton
gangs eager to make money by harvesting the precious potato, the
general use of such tools as spades and forks and hoes, and a steady
demand for all that could be exported despite the high production
costs due to the labour involved.

It was back to the tried and trusted old days of mixed farming
and crop rotations, with grass for pasture and hay, a few vergées
of oats or wheat, and as many vergées of spuds as possible followed
by turnips, swedes and mangolds as a second crop to feed a small
herd of cattle. The cows were milked by hand where they were
tethered in the field by day, or in the dusty, ill-lit stable where
they were housed at night.

In short, it was a return to what had come to be regarded
as the traditional style of Jersey farming which, despite demanding unending personal attention, had proved to be so profitable
for the smallholder's forefathers. Nobody in that brief, balmy postwar period of the late 1940s could have anticipated what was to
happen in the next two decades.

*   *   *

This is not the right place to dissect events and present them
in too close detail under the microscope of inquiry, although that
is a fitting analogy, for an old style of agriculture – indeed, a manner
of living stretching back through the generations which had done
so much to make Jersey special – was in the process of dying. An
education based on urban attitudes and a greater range of well-
paid career opportunities meant that many young Jerseymen, like
increasing numbers of Breton workers, no longer wanted to take
to the land. The Island's system of smallholder farming which had
evolved due to the presence of a plentiful supply of cheap family
labour was particularly badly hit by this drift away from the soil.

Those young people who stayed on the land were of a different sort from their parents. A natural reluctance to accept a lifetime of unending physical work, together with plain economic necessity, encouraged them to move to mechanisation. In turn that meant the need for larger farm units due to the capital costs involved. That fact alone began to put the Island's traditional system of small-scale farming under threat.

Troubles began to come from another direction. The immediate post-war boom led on to a decrease in the prices of, and the demand for, everything Island farmers produced, from cattle and potatoes to milk and tomatoes. For the ordinary smallholder, his milk cheque had once helped to pay some of the bills; now and again a heifer, a cow or a young bull might be sold overseas. But on the great majority of holdings the major sources of income had for long been the early potato and, where conditions were suitable, field-grown tomatoes. The financial returns from both crops were, as always, unreliable. While some years were good, others were poor; and the latter came to be the rule rather than the exception. Through a combination of thrift, few wants, an ability to live off the produce of their land and an acceptance of a particular way of life shared by most of their relations and friends, former generations had been able to ride out any bad times. During the prosperous period which stretched from the early 1800s right through to the outbreak of the Second World War, there was money enough and little cause to spend it.

But from 1950 onward things began to change. There was less available labour and less cash in the bank. One worked against the other. Labour shortages meant a need for capital investment in tractors and the equipment that goes with them, milking machines or a new lorry. There were expensive repairs and improvements to be made to buildings left untouched during the Occupation years. There was also a demand for a more sophisticated lifestyle that only wealth in the form of money could bring. In their homes the farming community, in common with everybody else, wanted bathrooms, carpets, refrigerators, washing machines – running water, even – holidays and those new television sets.

With a pig in the sty, fowls in the yard, potatoes in store, produce from a kitchen garden, milk coming twice a day to be drunk

145

fresh or turned into butter and cream, and perhaps even flour ground from home-grown wheat, at one time there might have been no great dependence on cash. But now it was essential, if only because of changes in society's perception of things. Willing or otherwise, the smallholder found himself caught up in the whirligig of cash economics. The trouble was that however much the farmer worked, there was no longer profit enough for a comfortable living to be made from holdings whose average size was a mere twenty-five vergées.

Above and beyond all these difficulties there lay one which was supreme. Many, perhaps the majority, of Jersey's older smallholders regarded their kind of farming as a way of life. They knew no other. Such men lacked the education, the flexibility or perhaps even the desire to adapt to the changing circumstances which, ever more tightly, were embracing so much of the western world. In this post-war period agriculture everywhere was truly becoming an industry whose prosperity, and maybe even survival, depended on mechanisation and low costs of production which were only possible by working on a larger scale and more efficiently. It also demanded the mind of a businessman rather than merely a love of the land, livestock and tradition.

*   *   *

The old way of Jersey farming – a little bit of this, some of that, all laboriously produced on a small scale – was no longer in a position to compete with the new methods being introduced elsewhere, or the subtle but increasing influences within the Island that were causing such profound changes in lifestyles. Among the latter, some might include the adoption of English attitudes which had little regard for the centuries of wisdom and experience of the Jersey smallholder. Some growers had the commercial shrewdness to see that was happening and could find the funds needed to meet a challenge never experienced before. They adopted the new methods, took over more land and bought the necessary equipment so that they could operate their expanded businesses at the level changing conditions seemed to demand. But for many others that proved impossible.

So it was that Jersey's agriculture underwent a revolution. It came silently, disregarded by the States and the public in general. There was no whisper of protest from those affected. It never occurred to them to object. One by one, smallholder farmers were forced out of business either through age, a lack of cash or a sense of hopelessness. A few committed suicide. The situation in which members of an older generation found themselves could only have been made more depressing by memories of the days of the splendid, settled prosperity they had known in their youth.

Save among the unrecorded reminiscences of individuals, there is no way to gauge the scale of the human hardships and sorrows that were involved. But simple statistics show what happened in practical terms. Where, for example, in 1956, there had been 1,865 separate farming units, there were in 1993 only about five hundred, with numbers falling annually and with farmers cultivating some ten thousand fewer vergées of land.

Liberal States help is given these days in several ways to ensure that Jersey's agriculture survives more or less in its present form, if only for the sake of maintaining the Island's unique rural appearance which proves so attractive to the tourist. About half the financial aid is given in the form of subsidies paid to growers and milk producers. They were made necessary when, in 1971, the Island decided not to become a full member of the European Community. Consequently, the local agricultural industry was denied the benefit of the support given by the EC to others in the Community. So in order that Jersey's farmers could be put on level pegging with their overseas competitors, the States were obliged to provide financial support. In 1993 alone that direct aid amounted to some £4m out of an overall budget for agriculture of just under £8m.

Essential though they were from the outset, these subsidies meant that for the first time the level of a farmer's prosperity – and just as importantly the direction in which the Island's agricultural industry was to go – began to depend on factors other than the innate vitality of the industry and the give and take of a free market system which had existed for so many centuries previously. Where once there had been only the resourcefulness and enterprise of the individual to ensure his prosperity, there was now a quite

147

new regime of control and a necessary dependence on the continuing provision of public money.

The result of such a fundamental shift in any industry must at the very least be to alter the perspectives of those involved in it. And it has to be added that, although from the best of intentions, these subsidies have all along tended to benefit those who produced the most for export – that is, farmers with the most land. That was yet another factor in the demise of the Island's particular form of agriculture based entirely on the smallholder.

*   *   *

It is too easy to criticise events from a safe distance in time. Even though it lagged behind changes going on in the rest of Western Europe by a decade or two, Jersey's agricultural revolution during the years after the Occupation was inevitable. Besides, it coincided with the consequences flowing from Britain's entry into the Common Market, the boom in tourism in Jersey which followed the introduction of the cheap package holiday, and the explosive development in the Island of the finance industry.

Where once farming had (if only by long tradition) been top of the league in terms of public recognition, it quickly fell to a poor and disregarded third. Indeed, during most of the revolutionary years a farming community composed in part of a diminishing number of smallholders struggling for a living was more criticised than pitied for the plight it was in. Ignorant of the true situation, many said that in giving up his land and sometimes even the home where he and his forebears had been born, the greedy farmer was selling his birthright for cash. Few realised that financially there was no other choice. Whatever conclusions future historians reach about events during those two decades, in that short time a millennium of a system of farming peculiar to Jersey and which had done so much to create the character of the idiosyncratic Jerseyman was swept away.

Quite quickly, the smallholding began to vanish, and with it the smallholder. It was a profound, perhaps historically important, change. For it was the smallholders, held together by their own language and traditions, and sheltering in the final but ultimately vulnerable fortress of the countryside as might others in a mountain fastness, who had composed the last nucleus of the truly aboriginal people of Jersey. Deprived of their land and their freedom as self-employed citizens, they had themselves no choice but to change. As they went, or were absorbed into the new postwar society, something of the Island community that was quite irreplaceable went with them.

In their place came another kind of farmer – perhaps even another kind of person – and a style of agriculture on a much grander scale, more technical, more similar to that found in England; and perhaps with less respect for the soil and certainly with less thought for the wisdom, knowledge and experience acquired by past generations.

Maybe all that was inevitable and right. On the other hand the wisdom of hindsight returns to suggest that something might have been done to encourage the smallholder to survive, as farming itself is now being helped to survive, if only as a natural and beneficial part of the fabric of Island life. But that was not to be. Until the consequences of staying outside the Common Market led to the need for government aid, the idea of providing the crutch of subsidies for any industry judged to be unable to stand on its own two feet of vitality and profit was not one Jersey politicians would have been prepared even to consider.

Seen from this moment in history, the outlook for Jersey agriculture in its present form can hardly be said to be cheerful, despite the support it receives. That seems to be a view shared by many members of the farming community, whose numbers are shrinking annually. It is almost as though the good fortune which had dogged the small rural world of Jersey right from the growth of the knitting trade in the early 1500s has finally gone away, or anyway transferred itself to other aspects of Island life through the newly-discovered finance industry.

*   *   *

The last time fortune smiled on the smallholder, it did so briefly – and then only on those who were the owners and occupiers of their properties. During this postwar period of rural turmoil there arrived an influx of wealthy immigrants looking for smart country homes. They found them in many of Jersey's lovely granite-built, slate-roofed, Regency-style farm houses and their extensive outbuildings and gardens. So far as their proprietors were concerned, they had become far too big, too run down and too costly to maintain from the profits to be extracted from the parcels of land that went with them. The immigrants were willing buyers. A number of owners, willing or otherwise, were sellers.

Many of these fine properties had been built in the great days of farming made hugely prosperous by cider, cattle, potatoes and tomatoes – and the wealth which came to families through their seafaring relatives. In a way, they may have been regarded then as status symbols. In the 1960s they were to become so again, but this time for a very different kind of Island inhabitant.

Inscribed in Latin on one of the walls of St Paul's Cathedral in London, obviously referring to its architect, Sir Christopher Wren, there are the words *Si monumentum requiris, circumspice* ('If you seek a monument, look around you.') It is surely not stretching sentimentality to breaking point to suggest that, refurbished and cared for, these delightful buildings (which convinced John Stead a hundred and fifty years earlier that the 'Erector had built not only for himself but for his Posterity') remain as visible monuments to a past age that cannot return; and to a truly singular breed of Jersey men and women – descendants of the Island's original inhabitants and their way of life – now either absorbed into another age or all but vanished.

*   *   *

In all records of this kind there has to come a point at which the story must end. It is appropriate that this one should end in the 1960s, because it was there that the events which form the small stream of Jersey's history took a sharp turn. It was during this decade that the Island finally ceased to be predominantly rural and attractively remote but instead became both urban and anglicised.

There have been many changes to Jersey's agricultural industry since the 1960s which have no place here, significant

'The Erector had built not only for himself but his Posterity.'

though they have been. But the stream of history continues to flow, taking with it a part of what it has gathered in the past and carrying it beyond the present into the future.

The Island and the way of life of its inhabitants are not now what they once were. That does not make either Jersey or its people in the last years of the millennium worse or necessarily better in every respect. Nor does it mean that change and the dilution that is the result of immigration have by themselves altered the fundamental character and temperament of a small community. Jersey remains inescapably bound to the influence of times past to a greater extent than many other regions simply by virtue of long ages of self-determination and the natural cohesiveness to be found among all island populations. Moreover, if history has a value, it must surely be to provide a perspective and a basis for understanding, not a reason for mourning and regret.

13.
The Twilight of Jèrriais
by Max Lucas

IN HIS FOREWORD to Paul Birt's *Lé Jèrriais Pour Tous*, former Bailiff of Jersey Sir Frank Ereaut quotes the famous Dr Johnson as saying that languages are the pedigree of nations. The Jersey language had served Jerseymen as their ordinary means of communication for centuries, said Sir Frank. 'But it is much more than that. It is the repository of life and thoughts of our Island people. Their long and vibrant history, their remarkable achievements and their sturdy independence of character are all reflected in the richness of its idiom and vocabulary.'

Sir Frank added that Paul Birt's grammar and textbook would 'surely encourage many .... to learn or re-learn our highly expressive and robust insular tongue, and so ensure its survival and, indeed, revival'. He was writing in 1985. Four years later the Jersey census showed that only 5,720 people (under seven per cent) of the Island population of nearly 83,000 spoke Jersey Norman-French, and of these as many as 89 per cent were aged sixty or over. Fewer than one per cent were under the age of fifteen.

Giving these figures in *A Brief History of Jèrriais* (published in 1993), Professsor N.C.W. Spence wrote: 'Fifty years ago Jèrriais was still widely spoken in most of the country parishes, especially those in the north of the Island which remained primarily agricultural. Compared to the regional vernaculars of Normandy, to which Jèrriais is related, it seemed to be maintaining itself well.'

However, the use of the language that had developed in isolation for over seven hundred years since King John lost continental Normandy rapidly declined in the years after the

German Occupation as the people who spoke it, and the way of life it so expressively reflected, were submerged by the influx of an 'alien' culture that was predominantly of the United Kingdom and Ireland.

But had anybody who came to Jersey as a visitor during the first half of this century walked along a country lane they would almost certainly have heard a tongue unfamiliar to them being spoken by people working in the fields or farmyards. Jersey Norman-French would also have been heard during a stroll around St Helier, especially in or near the markets or the agricultural merchants' stores which then lined the Esplanade.

That language – so useful during the Occupation years because it was unintelligible to the Germans – was not, and is not, 'a barbarous dialect of French'. It is a vernacular as old as the mixture which became the official language of France through that historical chance whereby the central governing power came to be established in the Paris region, where the dominant tongue was Francien.

This, as Norman or Picard, was a vernacular of the *langue d'oïl*, the evolution in Northern France of what had been vulgar Latin as opposed to the growth of the *langue d'oc* in the south of France. (*Oïl* and *oc* were different pronunciations of the word for 'yes'.)

Jèrriais is, then, a branch of the Norman *langue d'oïl*. It is akin to the Cotentin *parler* of north Coutançais. Guernesiais, on the other hand, is closer to the particular and more northern *parler* of La Hague.

Because of the Island's long period of geographical and political isolation from the influences of the King's English on the one hand and the King's French on the other, Jèrriais was able to maintain its originality and vitality for a considerable period of time. Vitiation – mainly from English, partly from French – came comparatively late in the life of the Island language.

The 'contamination' – this addition of French and English words used in Jersey Norman-French – is often a cause for derision among the uninformed. But, for example, one has only to open an English dictionary and note the number of words 'borrowed' from the French language and others to understand that all languages are a 'contaminated' mix derived from many sources.

There are other detractors of the local vernacular who claim that it cannot be a language because it has no literature. They fail to realise that many a native tongue spoken over much greater areas than Jersey have been turned into written form only in comparatively recent years. This did not make them any the less languages in their own right during the many hundreds of years in which they existed solely in the form of speech.

Besides, there is in fact a wealth of literature in Jersey Norman-French, dating though it does only to the first half of the nineteenth century. And it was from the Channel Islands that the great effusion of Norman literature of this period first appeared, pre-dating that of the Cotentin peninsula of Normandy.

Indeed, Jersey can lay claim to much earlier fame, for one of the greatest of the Romance poets of the twelfth century was Maistre Wace. At one point in the more than sixteen thousand lines of his *Roman de Rou*, a chronicle of the Dukes of Normandy from the time of the Norse chieftain Rollo, Wace stresses from where he came:

> *Jo di è dirai ke jo sui*
> *Wace de l'isle de Gersui*

'I'll say, and will say, that I am Wace from the island of Jersey.'

In *Jersey:An Isle of Romance*, Blanche B. Elliott says that the Roman de Rou is 'claimed as the first national epic of modern Europe'. Be that as it may, Wace was perhaps the foremost of his day to contribute to the explosion of what was becoming a literary language, much of which was Norman.

Seven centuries or so later, when there was this second out-pouring of kindred literature, one comes to the works, among others, of such Jerseymen as the elegiac poet Henri Luce Manuel (1818-1875). Typical of his verse is this from *Leignes à m'n êfant qui veint d'mouori* (Lines to my child who has just died).–

Touot est finni. La vallée dé la mort
La v'là pâssée. Lé souffrant à ch't heu dort.
Pus d'cris, ni r'gards, ni lèrmes d'agonie
N'y a pas à souffri iou n'y a pus la vie.
Oh, Dgieu mèrci,
Touot est finni!

'It is all over. The valley of death/Is passed. Now the sufferer sleeps./ No further cries, or looks, or tears of agony./ There's no suffering where there's no longer life./Oh praise God,/It is all over!'

Then, too, as Maurice Piron has it in his *Les Littératures Dialectales du Domaine d'Oïl,* there were 'the minor masterpieces of emotion and tenderness' of Sir Robert Pipon Marett (1820-1884).

But by no means all that has been written in Jersey Norman-French is of a serious nature. Humour abounds, as it does in the spoken word itself. As a typical example, what the *Jersey Evening Post* (the Island's 'national daily') called one of the best stories in Jèrriais (*ieune des miyeuthes histouaithes en Jèrriais*) appeared in its columns in April, 1986. It repeated the tale of how Centenier Bram Bilo (Abraham Billot), the creation of Philippe Le Sueur Mourant (1848-1918), went to a farm sale and ended up owning an unwanted wheelbarrow, a *chiviéthe,* a *païle* – the huge brass vessel in which *nièr beurre* (black butter) is made – and a nag. Because he blinked the wheelbarrow was knocked down to him. Similarly he acquired the *païle* because he coughed, and the nag because he spat.

Twice the auctioneer asked for confirmation of sale from the onlookers, who were only too willing to have a bit of fun at the expense of a parish official. As the story goes: *Véthe! véthe! il a toussu,' tch'i' disent tous, 'il a toussu.'*('Yes! yes! he coughed,' they all said, 'he coughed.'

Dr Roger Jean Lebarbenchon, who is highly placed in the French educational training profession, realising that the native literature of the Channel Islands and the Cotentin is 'one of the richest in the domain of the *langue d'oïl,*. completed a thesis on the subject in 1982.

In a subsequent book, *La Grève de Lecq*, Dr Lebarbenchon deals with the poets and writers already mentioned, and a dozen or so more, including Mrs Amelia Perchard. He then covers in detail the works of Dr Frank Le Maistre and George Francis Le Feuvre. The latter had more than nine hundred articles in Jèrriais published as regular contributions in the *Jersey Evening Post* under the *nom de plume* George d'La Forge. Of this formidable output, Dr Lebarbenchon wrote that it elevated 'his testimony to the rank of a Jersey epic'.

Dr Frank Le Maistre's major work is undoubtedly the unique *Dictionnaire Jersiais-Français*, which standardized the orthography of Jèrriais. It, and his other works – especially his interpretation of the Rubáïyát of *Omar Khayyám* – have earned widespread acclaim and honour for the author.

The dictionary is not merely a dictionary. It is also a repository of local idioms, sayings, proverbs and folklore. As one example, while this chapter was being written a whirlwind occurred a mile or so away. Looking up the equivalent – *la folle d'avoût* or *la vielle d'avoût* (the crazy woman of the harvest) – in the dictionary, one learns that this phenomenon was thought to be caused by a fairy or pixie trying to snatch up the harvest. There was only one thing to do: grab a hay-fork or a knife and hurl it at the turbulence.

A whirlwind was also described as *la fil'ye d'Hérode tchi châque ses cotillons* – Herod's daughter shaking her skirts.

Substituting Jèrriais for Cotentinais in an extract (in translation) from the preface to André J. Desnouettes' *L'Epopée Cotentine*: 'Jèrriais is a language capable of expressing every sentiment. It is incredibly rich and of a correctness of use not often found.'

For example, one might say of a woman soon to give birth: *Ou s'en va bein vite faithe pieds neufs* – (she'll very soon make new feet); or of a woman who has died of old age: *Oulle est morte dé sa belle mort* – she died of her fine death.

While English or French words were sometimes incorporated, the Jersey Norman-French language has a very large vocabulary that can be used to provide a great range of nuances. There are, for instance, at least twenty-five words that can be used to describe a physical blow, from *brûlée* to *tournéoualipe*.

In their day-to-day conversations, the Jersey people could also make use of hundreds of proverbs and sayings, many of them to do with country life. *Nou n'graisse pon la tèrre auve des fièrs dé tchéthue* (ploughing does not manure the land). Or: *Y'a juge dé bête, et bête dé juge* (there are judges of beasts and fools of judges – a play on the word *bête*, which can mean either beast or fool. The remark can be used as a cynical comment on the decisions of cattle show judges). As to outright derision: *Tchi mathyie eune Dgèrnésiaise né s'sa janmais à s'n aise* (he who marries a Guernseywoman will never be at ease – a reflection of the animosity which has existed from ancient times between Jersey and Guernsey). Or again: *À janne femme et vièr baté, y'a tréjous tchiquechose à calfaîter* (a young woman and an old boat always need attention).

This short article can provide but a mere taste of the stuff and richness of which Jèrriais is made. As a separate language it has perhaps outlived the way of life of which it was the daily medium of expression. It no longer nurtures a culture stretching back a thousand years.

Written Jèrriais is mainly perpetuated in a quarterly publication, *Les Nouvelles Chroniques du Don Balleine*, which won the 1993 Prix Littéraire du Cotentin. The spoken word, in its variety of parochial dialects, can on occasions still be heard in town and country, and briefly every Sunday in a five-minute programme on Radio Jersey. But as Dr Le Maistre wrote nearly half a century ago: '(Jersey) will be anglicised and modernised, systemised and standardised.'

Wace, centuries ago, could hardly have foreseen in particular the twilight years of what had been his mother tongue. But what he did affirm in an all-embracing threnody was that:

> *Tute rien se turne en déclin,*
> *Tut chiet, tut muert, tut vait à fin*
>
> *All things to nothingness descend,*
> *Everything falls, dies, comes to an end*

Thus it must be with the ancient language of the Island people, a force which once sustained the singularity of Jersey itself.

PRINCIPAL REFERENCE SOURCES

Balleine's History of Jersey (revised by Syvret and Stevens), (Phillimore and Co Ltd).

Old Jersey Houses (vols 1 and 2); Joan Stevens; (Phillimore and Co Ltd).

English Social History; G.M. Trevelyan; (Longman Ltd).

Black's Veterinary Dictionary; A and C. Black.

Cattle of the World: John B. Friend; (Blandford Press).

The Jersey Cow and its Island Home: Elisabeth Le Ruez, 1992; (produced for the Royal Jersey Agricultural and Horticultural Society).

Jersey: Ile Agricole Angle-Normande; Dr Pierre Dalido, 1951; (Imprimerie Chaumeron, Vannes).

The Island of Jersey Today; R.C.F. Maugham (1939); (W.H. Allen).

A Picture of Jersey; John Stead; (La Haule Books Ltd).

Jersey in the 15th-18th Centuries (3 vols); A.C. Saunders; (J.T. Bigwood Ltd).

The Channel Islands; D.T. Ansted and R.G. Latham; (Wm Allen and Co, 1862).

The Channel Islands: Henry Inglis, 1835 (available at La Société Jersiaise reference library)

Queen of the Isles: 'A Twenty Years Resident', 1840; (as above).

The Channel Islands: Edward T. Gastineau, 1858; (as above).

The Channel Isles and Islanders: 'DFS', 1882; (as above).

Jersey Potato Exports in the 19th Century: thesis by K.P. Durtnall; (as above).

Bulletins of La Société Jersiaise.

Statistics published by the Department of Agriculture, Jersey.

L'Epopée Cotentine: André J. Desnouettes; (Editions OCEP, 1968).

Jersey: an Isle of Romance: Blanche B. Elliott; (T. Fisher Unwin Ltd, 1923).

Les Littératures Dialectales Du Domaine d'Oïl: (Gallimard, Paris, 1978).

La Grève de Lecq, Les Chansons des Assemblées, Les Falaises de la Hague: Roger Jean Lebarbenchon; (various publishers).

Dictionnaire Jersiais-Français: Dr Frank Le Maistre; (Don Balleine Trust, Jersey).

Lé Jèrriais pour tous; Paul Birt; (Don Balleine Trust).

A Brief History of Jèrriais: N.C.W. Spence; (Don Balleine Trust).

Les Nouvelles Chroniques du Don Balleine: (Don Balleine Trust).